Spirit Talks

Book One

with Paulette

Published by Paulette Watts 2019

Copyright © 2019 Paulette Watts

All rights reserved. No part of this publication may be reproduced, stored in a retrieval system, or transmitted in any form or by any means, electronic, mechanical, photocopying, recording or otherwise, without the prior written permission from the publisher.

Disclaimer

Every effort has been made to ensure that this book is free from error or omissions. Information provided is of general nature only and should not be considered legal or financial advice. The intent is to offer a variety of information to the reader. However, the author, publisher, editor or their agents or representatives shall not accept responsibility for any loss or inconvenience caused to a person or organisation relying on this information.

A catalogue record for this book is available from the National Library of Australia.

Book cover design and formatting services by SelfPublishingLab.com

www.spirittalks.com.au

ISBN:
978-0-9876453-0-2 (pbk)
978-0-9876453-1-9 (e-bk)

Acknowledgements

This book would not be possible without the encouragement and insight of two incredible women, Lilian Parrish and Trudy Grant. It is due to their unwavering belief in me, and their own connection to Spirit, that this book came into existence.

I am also very grateful for the support of my two children, Samantha and Jessica, and special thanks to Kylie Mathison and Helen Rajkovich.

Special mention to all my friends and clients that have encouraged me on this journey especially, Lynda Robinson who did the illustrations for the book, Dale Oria who designed the Spirit Talks logo, Michelina Dichiera, Christina Foundas, Judy and Michael Klobas, Monica Cook, Alex Conlon, and Paula McMahon.

Thank you for everything.

Contents

Acknowledgements	iii
Foreword by Paulette	vii
The Collective: A few opening words	x
1 The Collective	1
2 Your Divine Spark	4
3 Why Now?	8
4 Activating the New Energy	12
5 Feelings	16
6 Living in the Now	21
7 Who You Really Are	26
8 The Business of Life	30
9 This is the Time	37
10 Energy	42
11 The Birthing of the Planet	45
12 You are the New Energy	53
13 You are Renewed	59

14 The Power of Intention	64
15 Positive Changes	68
16 The Importance of Choice	80
17 How to Release Soul Contracts and Karma	92
18 The Influence of Technology	96
19 The Source Chakra	101
20 Tending Your Aura	106
21 The Multiverse	113
22 How to Release Karma	117
23 The Positive Changes	122
24 In Summary	128
25 One Last Word	131
About Paulette	135
How I connect with Spirit	137

Foreword by Paulette

Spirit Talks was created by Spirit, a group of non-physical beings simply known as *The Collective*. I have been chatting with Them for many years, and They have become a natural and normal part of my life. I am very grateful for Their wisdom and support, and I do hope They become part of your daily life as well!

From the onset, it is stated many times that this book is an energy book and is a bit different to other books and information that is currently in circulation. *The Collective's* intention is so strong and so powerful that it cannot be anything less. As They were speaking to me and asking me to write the information, They ensured the ego part of me was certainly not present when I was conversing with Them. If my energy dropped, They would stop talking and only recommence when I could fully support Their energy. This is one of the reasons why this book took a little while to come to fruition, but why it is so powerful and transformative.

The Collective encouraged me to channel Their information as They wanted you to realise that now is the time for you to begin creating a life you truly desire. Never before in the history of the planet has our ability to change our reality been so readily available. This is due to the energy flowing into the planet that is unlike anything ever witnessed. It took me a while to understand that manifesting was very possible and very quick, for this seems at odds with what we are experiencing on a global scale. Yet, because of our planetary unrest, it is time for us to begin to create the very opposite of what we are witnessing. We are called to be the counterbalance to the planet's pain and to begin living a more authentic life based on our own reasoning and information rather than what is fed to us through media and the powerful organisations that have world dominance. So, to those who are aware of the power of intention and thought processes, it is your time to shine and to help others to connect more fully with their uniqueness. To those who are at the beginning of this planetary ride, I hope this book will be a catalyst for new understandings.

You will also notice that *The Collective* will encourage you to put down the book at certain stages as They know that you will need time to integrate the energy that is being delivered directly to you. From my own personal experience, I would heed Their advice, but, of course, They are respectful of your free will decisions (as they were of mine). Whatever you choose will be okay. The most important thing is that you have made a conscious choice to bring this book into your life.

My intention is that *Spirit Talks* awakens and activates you, for you are very much needed on this planet at this time. Now is not the time to hide but instead shine, and if your self-belief wavers, know that Spirit will hold it for you until you reclaim it again.

The Collective
A few opening words

Greetings to all you special souls that are choosing to read or listen to Our words. We are very happy to be able to impart Our knowledge and understanding to you via this book and have great faith that you will begin to create a happier life for yourself and those around you.

Our intention in creating this book is to assist you in remembering who you are and to activate your unique consciousness, which is capable of changing your reality. The time for remembering is **NOW**. The time for your personal activation is **NOW**. There is an urgency that can no longer be ignored regarding the state of your planet, and **YOU** are being asked to choose whether you want to experience more of the same for the coming years or not.

Each of you, at some level, are being called to lift your unique energy vibration so it can ripple out through this planet, shattering the illusions that have captivated, distracted, and disempowered the masses. You are being called to bring forth the *Creator Spark* so that it can work its magic and begin to create a world that sets you free.

Know that there is an urgency amongst Us as well. The decision that you all make regarding the direction of your planet will have an effect on Our universe and existence. We are inexorably linked to the energy of your planet. What you choose will affect Us and Our desire to be whole expressions of the Creator. For Us to flourish your world is required to bring in the higher vibrational frequency that is been offered in this very moment. We have experienced this frequency and have evolved considerably, and We now wait the next level of energy consciousness. We cannot, however, have full access to this consciousness until your planet ignites the frequency. It is the same for energy beings that are of a higher consciousness than Us. They await to meet an even higher frequency but are in a holding mode until We shift. Can you see the pattern? Were you aware of this truth?

Thus, there are many non-physical beings that are very invested in the energy of your planet and have come to assist as much as they are allowed. We say to you, there are many who also do not desire a more positive change and wish the planet to remain in a lower vibrational frequency. As you battle there on Earth, We battle here in the sky and the universe for freedom of expression, as opposed to slavery of the soul.

So, We invite you to read on. Already you have commenced the awakening process just by reading these words; such is the power of this book and its intention.

Know that We are here for you and will answer any questions you may have as you experience the energy of this book. We will always endeavour to communicate with you and all that is asked is that you listen and feel for Us.

Now, let Us begin.

CHAPTER ONE

The Collective

Welcome to *Spirit Talks*.

We are very happy to open Our conversation with you by introducing Ourselves. We are known as *The Collective* and We are a vast array of beings that are here to assist your planet and its inhabitants at this very crucial time. You may have noticed that your world is in an apparent state of disarray and confusion. We see this very clearly and are very concerned at this state of affairs. We are also very aware that amongst this topsy-turvy time there is an influx of energies beaming down to your planet that is both enlightening and transformative. This new energy is the reason for why We can communicate and assist you as a doorway has opened for *The Collective* to enter and offer help.

Our words with you may be both enlightening and disquieting at different points. This is why We suggest that, at certain times, you put down this book while you ingest the information and the energy it holds. This is an energy book, and it is impossible for you not to be affected by the information it contains. That is why this book was created. It is intended to bring change to your lives that in turn will have a domino effect on the lives of the people around you and, of course, the planet.

We will often refer to two different energies. The first energy is termed the *older energy* or *controlling energy*. This is the low vibrational frequency energy that has kept the planet and its inhabitant's captive for thousands of years. This is the energy that is responsible for the way the planet has evolved during this time. It is based on control, greed, manipulation, lies, and fear. It has contained little empathy or thought and is the energy that has dominated and contaminated the masses. It is used by those in positions of power to create misery and pain.

The second energy we refer to is the *new* and *emergent energy*. It reverberates at a much higher frequency and is infiltrating the planet at this time to assist in lifting the Earth from a seething mass of lower vibrational consciousness to

CHAPTER ONE: THE COLLECTIVE

a state of higher consciousness. There is a small window of opportunity for this to occur, and it requires many individuals to raise their vibrational frequency to create this change. This window of opportunity is between 2013 and 2027 Earth years. This is how much time you have to bring about a positive change, which has the power to transcend your current life.

We will refer many times to your free will. As humans, you each possess free will. This has been decreed by the Creator and, thus, is universal law. However, you will discover that time and time again, your free will choices have been manipulated and controlled, and, as a result, you have created a life based on fear that perfectly suited the controlling energy.

Now, the very BIG thing that has happened, that has struck much excitement and awe amongst Us, is the relighting of your divine spark!

Let Us tell you about it.

CHAPTER TWO

Your Divine Spark

Your divine spark is your own unique frequency or energy. It is the expression of the Creator and all beings, from every multiverse and dimension, are divine sparks of the Creator. To be more precise: everything that is anything and anything that is everything is part of the Creator.

What has changed for you on your planet is that your divine spark has been relit or reignited. In other words, your unique frequency has undergone a shift that creates the opportunity for you to wake up and activate the part of you that has been dormant and suppressed. Your divine

CHAPTER TWO: YOUR DIVINE SPARK

spark is now vibrating at a higher level-you are vibrating at a higher level. This is to help you remember who you really are. For you, as an expression of Source, have forgotten. As a result, you have disconnected from yourself and have felt separated from Source.

Now may be a good time to place the book aside and sit for a while. Your divine spark was relit as soon as you became aware of this book's existence. Such is the power of Our intention that it cannot be otherwise. You are now a higher vibrational expression of Source. You have the opportunity to create a positive change for yourself by a higher awareness of the free will choices at your disposal. This is a BIG statement and, therefore, it may require a little time to process. If you feel the desire to pause and contemplate, then this is a good thing. If you are eager for more information, then read on. Whatever you choose is perfect for you.

Let Us further elaborate. This spark is your own unique energy. It is who you really are. It is how Spirit communicates with you and how you communicate with Spirit.

At this point upon the planet, there is an opportunity for every soul's life spark to be reignited. Yes, reignited. This book is one of the catalysts for this to take place. We have stated that your divine spark has been relit from the moment you became aware of this book. You have been reignited using the enormously powerful light energy present on this planet. This means that you are now able to hold within yourself the frequency of this light energy. Prior to this, your spark (your energy) was not quite strong enough to hold and use this higher vibrational frequency.

Let Us consider a few points. This planet, and the energies upon the planet, have become used to dealing with, living with, and creating with the same energy for thousands of years. You are now at the beginning of a new planetary cycle. This new cycle has the opportunity to be lighter, brighter, faster, and more complex in energetic vibration than ever experienced and such an energy has different requirements for each inhabitant. For planetary change to occur, the Creator has decreed that each soul's divine spark be relit so that these requirements are experienced. It is Our understanding that babies born from 2013 are of a higher vibrational frequency and instinctively feel the new energy. This is one of the reasons why many newborns and toddlers are very reactive to the environment and may experience a sensitivity to foods, medicines, preservatives, and environmental toxins such as radiation and pesticides. These children instinctively feel the artificiality of the world and bring attention to the need for a healthier way of living.

CHAPTER TWO: YOUR DIVINE SPARK

The wonderful thing is that once your divine spark has been relit, then YOU are the catalyst for other souls to experience this also. Yes! All those you love and have an affinity for will automatically undergo the relighting process. As soon as they come in contact with your energy field this will take place. That soul will now have the opportunity to shift their consciousness.

We have said that your free will choice will come into play here. You may have given him/her the opportunity to connect more fully and become the new energy, but it is up to that person to ultimately choose to take advantage of this amazing opportunity.

What may occur is the receiving soul may feel more inclined to begin questioning areas in his/her life that he/she never considered before. An awareness comes into play. He/she may not understand this subtle change of attitude, but needless to say, the opportunity to bring positive change is at the ready. Never before in your planet's history has this event come about, but such is the manipulation and distortion of your world that great steps have been taken to help shift mass consciousness.

CHAPTER THREE

Why Now?

Now We hear you ask, 'Why has it taken so long for this to occur? Can the Creator not see what is happening?'.

Our answer to this question is that, to bring about change, souls upon your planet had to ask for assistance. It has had to reach such a point that some of the populace are using their free will to ask for help. Your planet has had to reach such a state, such a lower energetic vibration, that it has affected you to such an extent that you now want change!

We have observed that humans are quite content to let things remain the same as long as it does not affect you

CHAPTER THREE: WHY NOW?

or your well-being. Oh, you have heard, read, and seen diabolical situations through your television and media outlets, but they are a world away, and you can switch off or change the channel. You have become much like the electronics you rely on: your consciousness switches off to the poverty, disease, corruption, and greed that inundate your existence every second of every day. You have begun to act like an electronic device.

You receive programs (data) from your government, banking systems, medical, and pharmaceutical industries. You do not question but simply apply this data and then run the program (your life) from this information. Sometimes it has worked, but, most often, there is a virus that penetrates and tries to completely erase all your former programs, and you have to rebuild yourself again. Each time you do so, you have to contend with all forms of malware, and you become run down. In the end, you cannot be rebuilt or rebooted, and so you end up on the scrap heap.

We use this analogy to help you understand two main points. Firstly, that you have become robotic in your reaction to world horrors, and secondly, your reliance on electronic devices is not one of balance or health. As a result, the help and assistance that has always been waiting in the wings could not be activated and used until now.

It has taken a certain percentage of the population to lift their vibrational frequency or, in other words, to begin using their own data and not outside influences to begin the change.

Can you understand now? Can you sense the truth in Our words? Our intention is not to criticise or judge but rather to help you understand why the time is now for the change to occur.

The relighting of your divine spark provides an opportunity for you to connect with the new energies flowing into the planet, thus helping you create a far more authentic and powerful life by truly seeing how your reality has been duped. You have the power to help others do the same. For many of you reading and listening to Our words, you feel an innate desire to assist humankind on some level.

You also have the ability to communicate with non-physical beings in a simpler fashion. It is no longer necessary for you to create a sacred space or use other practices to communicate with Spirit. This is because the relighting of your divine spark has automatically lifted your energetic vibration to such an extent that you can communicate with Spirit anytime and anywhere! We encourage you to do this as often as possible and particularly during any anxious moments you may experience. Spirit will do their utmost to

CHAPTER THREE: WHY NOW?

ensure you receive comfort, information, and healing during these times.

If you still feel the desire to cleanse a space, use crystals, or repeat a mantra, then We encourage you to do so. Our emphasis is solely on how much simpler it is now to connect with non-physical beings. We understand this may be helpful to know as many souls are busy with day to day living.

CHAPTER FOUR

Activating the New Energy

How are you feeling? More positive or are you still pondering Our information? We say to you that if you are questioning, then this is a very good thing. For too long many of you have stopped questioning. So if you have commenced this process now, We are happy. If you feel you require some time to digest this information, then this may be a good time to leave this book be for a while. Otherwise, We invite you to read on as We discuss this new energy.

CHAPTER FOUR: ACTIVATING THE NEW ENERGY

We have briefly mentioned that there is an incredible surge of energy flowing into your planet at this current time. It is now a wonderful opportunity for you to become acquainted with this energy. Remember, you have just reignited your divine spark, and it is ready to take flame. To do this, fill yourself up with some of this energy. This will come from a happy memory that you hold and is imprinted in your being. It can be a memory of an event, a person, an animal, anything, as long as this bought joy and happiness to your being and you can recall it easily. The first thought that comes to mind is a good place to start this process.

Let Us begin.

Breathe. Hold this happy thought and truly feel it flow through your body until it settles in the area just beneath your heart. This is the lighting point for your spark. You may feel a warmth here as you process this energy. This warmth may then be felt travelling towards your stomach area as your spark begins to glow and gain strength. This is a good thing because the new energy resonates more to the heart and stomach area.

You may be aware of the chakras within the body. They are the energy centres of your physical body, and each chakra vibrates at a different frequency and emits a different colour. This has been confirmed by the use of aura imaging devices. The chakras are integral to the human form, for they are part of your ability to access a higher consciousness. The clearer the chakras, the more spiritually balanced you are.

The activation of the heart and the solar plexus chakra (the heart and the stomach respectively) will assist you in creating your own unique happiness from this moment. In the past, these two chakras and two areas of the body (your heart and stomach) were under duress. This is because the controlling energy honed in on the vulnerable areas of your being. The heart that allowed love, compassion, understanding, and peace to flow, and your stomach that allowed your own personal power and sense of self to shine through. These two chakras were very much under assault, hence heart and stomach attacks that could leave you feeling weak and unable to draw strength and nourishment from the life and food around you.

Can you see why the new energy is automatically drawn to these two areas in your body? This energy is about healing and restoring. Can you feel this happening inside your being? Can you feel the heat in your body, and can you sense a vibration that is spreading within? Can you feel a stirring of excitement or anticipation, or can you simply feel your body start to relax?

If you feel some sensation at this point this is, again, a good thing. It means your spark is firing. If you feel

CHAPTER FOUR: ACTIVATING THE NEW ENERGY

nothing, then this is ok. There is still a stirring of energy in your being that will be felt by you in due course, so please do not think you are doing anything wrong. We say to you, that there is no incorrect way to experience this process!

CHAPTER FIVE

Feelings

How do you feel now? Do you feel the urge to put down the book and just sit for a bit? Pat the dog or scratch the cat's ears? Hug someone you love? Or do you want to read on and discover more?

The point is, after you have read these words, you will want to do something happy and peaceful. Did you find yourself smiling at some point? Are you smiling now? If you felt a yes to any of these questions, then you are beginning to connect more fully with the new energy. The word *felt* is used deliberately here. You *feel* with the new emergent energy rather than think with it.

CHAPTER FIVE: FEELINGS

If you feel that you have not fully activated the energy within you, then repeat the process at another time. You can do this as many times as you desire. In time, this energy will automatically be flowing through you, and you can call on it instinctively when required.

We now wish to consider feelings.

Feelings. What does this word mean, and how has it affected you up to this point in your life? For you to have picked up this book and read this far means that somewhere along the line your feelings have created a sense of sadness within your being. This sad feeling may have seemed as if your divine spark was blown out for a time and only darkness existed. It amplified your fears and insecurities, helping you to feel small and powerless. The controlling energy was resonating very strongly with you, and you resonated very strongly with it. This was a two-way relationship, which yielded very little in the way of power and transformation.

Are you remembering now the times when you have felt sad? Have you felt the change in your being? A heaviness, lethargy, a race of the heartbeat, or the lowering of the head? Even a frown or furrowed brow? If you have, then this is good. You are reactive to the energy being emitted to you just from these words. How powerful is this? Words on a page that evoke feelings of fear or sadness?

How reactive are the cells in your body to this feeling? They are shrinking, trying to hide and take cover. They are trying to become smaller. They are copying you when you are faced with a fearful experience as you try to become smaller and hidden so the impact is not as great. Through fear, you may have gone another way. You may have become vicious with your words or even your own body. Either way, in that moment, both reactions are indicative of trying to hide and cover the real you.

Enough now. Let Us take a moment to reset the energy. Breathe in and out deeply three times, and feel the new energy wash over you again.

The new emergent energy quickly transmutes past angry and sad feelings. This is how strong and powerful it is. Remember that this energy is within you. It has been relit and reignited. It is now infusing your very being. This is very good, for it will help stabilise you during times of turbulence. It is very heart-centred and will often be felt around this area in the form of heat or even pulsations. Be aware of it. Draw it upward through your throat should you need to speak honestly and clearly about something, or draw it down towards your stomach area should you want to be strong in a situation. It will guide you in your actions and your words, creating a positive outcome for you and those around you.

CHAPTER FIVE: FEELINGS

This is why feelings are very important in using this energy. You are here on this planet, at this time, experiencing a myriad of emotions. You are supposed to feel sad, fearful, angry, and stressed as this is part of your humanity, part of your humanness. What is not supposed to happen is that you become part of the sad, fearful, angry, stressed experience for far, far too long. So long in fact that you become the experience and operate from it. In turn, the controlling energy fed your experience and made it bigger, better, and more dramatic, which created more of the sad, fearful, angry, and stressed experience. Can you see the cycle? Can you feel the power of it? It is a form of madness. But now this madness is coming to an end.

The emergence of this new energy and the relighting of your divine spark means that stressful experiences are not the dominant emotions in your life. You feel them, but you no longer stay in them and become one with them. You move through them with a fluidity unlike anything before this time, motivated to find happiness and become it. The emergent energy demands this from you. It will accept nothing less. The time for creating a life that comes from pain and fear is no more. The time for creating a better and more evolved version of yourself from the happiness in your life is now!

How does this feel? Are you excited? Are you smiling? Are you feeling a sense of relief? Do you feel better?

Now may be the time to put down the book and just allow this to sink in and integrate within you. You may want to sit quietly or give a big whoop in the air, journal an entry, contact a friend or loved one. Whatever you choose to do, it will be a happy activity. Alternatively, with a more curious mind, you may wish to read on and see what else transpires.

CHAPTER SIX

Living in the Now

It is time for you to begin living and creating in the ***Now*** moment. You have been conditioned to consider the future with intense scrutiny rather than living in the ***Now*** of your life. The ***Now*** is all that exists in the moment. The future is something that has taken form *only in your mind*. Often, your decision-making is based on something that might happen or is expected to happen at some point in the future. It is interesting that many of you live for the future rather than in the ***Now*** moment of your life. This was very intentionally encouraged by the people you interact with, the TV shows you watch, the social media you devote so much attention to, and, of course, the people in positions of authority that presume to know best.

You are encouraged to take out insurance policies to protect yourself from possible future demise, have medical needles to protect yourself from possible future disease outbreaks, to place your hard-earned money into financial institutions to provide for your future retirement, to arm yourself with weapons because of possible future invaders.

Can you see the pattern here? It is prudent for you to ensure you are healthy and have income, but if your focus is on the future rather than living in the ***Now***, you may miss out on opportunities that come your way.

The controlling energy was very happy to accommodate this way of living and support you in feeling fearful and unhappy. It cleverly manipulated the way you see the world and what it has to offer. What is so liberating is that the emergent energy embraces the ***Now*** moment. This is all it seeks and reflects. There is immense power in living in the ***Now*** for it allows you to base your free will decision making on what is happening currently rather than what may happen. Your divine spark, relit and reignited using the new energy, will assist you in living in the ***Now*** moment in a more comfortable and secure fashion.

We will use this example. You want to buy a new home. You do not have much money for a deposit and

CHAPTER SIX: LIVING IN THE NOW

are worried that you cannot afford it. You currently have a roof over your head, food on the table, and you are working. If you focus on what you have and let go of the fear that you will not be able to afford a home, you will discover that your ability to own a home is within reach. The emergent energy is in resonance with your divine spark, and it is aimed at the positive manifestation of your desires. In this case, it is a home.

We know this is a simple example and not life-threatening. Yet there are people that are in dire need of water, food, and shelter. How does this concept affect them? It does not. You see, these people already live in the **Now** moment. Their **Now** moment is survival. They cannot consider the future as they are not sure if they will live. Their **Now** moment is the most precious of **Now** moments, as it is the most fragile. It is because of this fragility that you will find these people to be the most open-hearted and generous. They can offer the last of their food to someone who has even less than them as they know what it is like to have absolutely nothing.

You can assist those souls who are enduring poverty and disease by focussing your energy on creating an authentic and generous life for yourself and those around you. We understand this may sound selfish and self-absorbed. Our answer is this: as you lift your vibration and live more positively, you have the power to help others do the same in your social world. Those that you help to live a positive life have the opportunity to assist others to do the same and so it goes on. It is a ripple effect.

Positivity ripples across communities and people are motivated to bring help and healing to others and the world. As this ripple effect continues, there exists an opportunity for a person to become a public figure that draws attention to the hardship of others and can push for changes to happen on a global scale. This person, with their divine spark relit and the emergent energy driving and motivating them, can unite people together to create peace. It is by positively focussing on your ***Now*** that a positive planetary experience is created.

So, take a minute to sit with this concept. How does it feel to focus on only the ***Now*** moment? Does it feel scary and strange? If it does, then it may be time to put down the book and allow the energy of these words to seep deeper into your being.

If you are feeling more comfortable with the ***Now*** concept, then you are ready to put this into action. Begin using the phrases such as, 'Now is the time for me to look forward to seeing more money in my bank account', or 'Now is the time for me to let go of that person who is being unkind to me'. 'Now is the time for me to look for

CHAPTER SIX: LIVING IN THE NOW

another job' or 'I am looking forward to starting it'. Can you feel the positivity of these expressions?

The emergent energy feeds this positivity. It amplifies it. The controlling energy fed the negativity of your thoughts and actions and amplified those, too. Begin using your divine spark to create a life in the **Now** moment that will, in turn, create more positive life expressions.

As you begin to experience a happier life, you have the opportunity to assist those who are suffering the fragility of life. Perhaps you can help feed the homeless, donate foods and bedding to an animal shelter, train a guide dog, visit the elderly, or volunteer at a charity. There are many avenues to creating a better world.

CHAPTER SEVEN

Who You Really Are

Now that We have spoken to you about living in the *Now* moment, it is time to bring another concept to your mind about who you truly are. We understand you may have read, heard, and learned many schools of thought about who you are. This is another good thing, as it has opened your mind about the different possibilities that exist.

What We want you to consider is this: Who do you *feel* you are? Does this seem a strange and unfamiliar question? If you require time to think of the answer or if you have any difficulty in answering, then We suggest you put down

CHAPTER SEVEN: WHO YOU REALLY ARE

the book for the time being and *feel* your way to an answer – not think. If you need to think about the answer, this means that you have been conditioned to think of yourself more with the mind rather than the heart.

The mind is very easy to condition. All it requires is the same message being repeated numerous times until a belief system has been formulated. Once the formulation has taken place, the mind operates from this belief system. Whether the repeated messages have a positive vibration or less of a positive vibration is dependent on where the messages are coming from and how much you allow the message to define who you are. So, once again, if you have to *think* of who you are, then put down the book for a moment or two.

Are you back now? Again, We ask, 'Who do you feel you are?'. What is your response?

The truth is, there is no right or wrong answer to this question. You are who you choose to be in each moment you live on this planet. Each heartbeat is a choice of how you choose to express yourself. This is a good description: you are an expression of yourself based on what belief system you choose to operate from.

The divine spark is your true expression, for it is part of an energy that is all-encompassing, and there are no adequate words that can give meaning and expression to such an energy. The closest word to this energy is *God* or *Creator* but, even then, the word itself has been corrupted down through the ages. Be mindful that the energy itself has not been corrupted, for this is impossible. The meaning of the word attached to the energy has been corrupted.

You are in essence part of the Creator. *We are part of the Creator.* We are different expressions from the same Source. We encourage you to feel this truth. You are special and unique. There is no one else like you. You cannot be copied or cloned (no matter how hard humans try). The controlling energy encouraged the sameness concept. It encouraged you to be very much in the mainstream of things whether it was fashion to career, or marriage to parenthood. If you ventured outside the norm, you were branded dysfunctional.

Know that to be the same is actually quite difficult for you to achieve. You are not meant for sameness. Being unique is your natural state. Being the same as everyone else requires conditioning, and the controlling energy was an expert in the conditioning process. You only have to switch on the television to see this conditioning in progress. You are inundated with advertisements to buy this bag, wear this brand, drive this car, wear this hairstyle, and even to act in a certain way. The role models held in esteem by your young encourage them to focus on the

CHAPTER SEVEN: WHO YOU REALLY ARE

outer, illusory world. Very few public figures encourage freedom of thought and creative expression.

We encourage you to embrace your uniqueness and to see the power in this. See the uniqueness in those around you, and be happy for them. We encourage you to resist the desire to conform in a world that presents itself falsely. For this is why many of you harbour false illusions of yourself, especially when it comes to knowing who you really are.

Know that as you harness more of the emergent energy there will be less desire to fit in with those around you. You might find that your choice of friends and even family that you spend time with may not be as fulfilling as before. Television programs and social media may not appear as entertaining. You will automatically seek and be drawn to more like-minded souls. You may yearn for more heart-centred and authentic conversations. This is a good thing. It does not mean that you care less about your family and friends. It simply is an indication that you are seeking higher vibrational experiences. The emergent energy will naturally drive you towards this with a minimum of fuss or effort.

CHAPTER EIGHT

The Business of Life

Let Us now discuss this business of life and how it affects you. We use the word *business* deliberately as the life you have been experiencing is, more often than not, based on results and the bottom line. If you follow a certain structure and guideline that is based on other people's success, then it should give you success as well. If this does not happen then it means you have failed. You have failed the system and you are a failure. Does this not feel true?

Say, for example, you study for an exam. You read the same books, read the information given about the exam, and spend many hours studying the topic. You

CHAPTER EIGHT: THE BUSINESS OF LIFE

then translate, as best as possible, the information you have stored in your brain to the prepared questions on the paper/computer screen in front of you. You struggle a bit with this. You know the information is stored in your brain, but you find it difficult to give the required answer in a different format that will give you a pass and success. You get the exam back and find you did not pass. You may feel devastated, angry, and frustrated. Your happiness was squashed because you were unable to conform within the structured parameters of the institution that tells you whether or not you are a success. So many of you place yourselves in the 'I am a failure' category because of an outside assessment of your ability to correctly translate the subject matter in a particular way.

Here is another example: you meet someone and are attracted to them. You enjoy their company, and you develop strong feelings. Along the way, they begin suggesting to you that they prefer your hair to be worn in a different way and that a manicured appearance would be great. They may even hint at a better paying job or change of career. You are beginning to love them, and so you start to change yourself according to the other person's desire of who they want you to be. This becomes a regular occurrence until you transform yourself for them. You feel that an external force has a better understanding and deeper appreciation of who you are than yourself. If you do not conform or listen, then you are failing them in some way, and you do not want that. Then, somewhere along the way, you have feelings of uneasiness or a sense of sadness that begins to settle within you. This is because you have allowed yourself to conform to their wishes. You have allowed an external source to define who you are based on their assessment of you.

The controlling energy was very encouraging to those souls wanting to have more control over others. It encouraged you on a personal level to conform to others' wishes. The same is occurring on the public platform with the rise in political power and large corporations that seem to be quite influential and are extremely business based.

The emergent energy is very high vibrational and will begin to dismantle those organisations that are based on rigidity and personal profit. It is happening as you are reading this book, but, more importantly, it is happening inside of you. The business of you is undergoing a restructuring. The awareness of who you are is rising within and is being lovingly fed by the new energy. It will assist in helping you determine what feels right for you and what does not. You have begun the process. Just become aware of it happening.

'How?', you ask or even, 'I feel the same. How can I be sure it is happening?'.

CHAPTER EIGHT: THE BUSINESS OF LIFE

We say to you, begin taking notice of your external world and how you are feeling about it. Are you feeling the need to declutter? Do you feel that some of the stuff that is around you is not as important as it once was? Do you feel the need to simplify your life? Do you feel the desire to make some changes? Do you feel the desire to eat certain foods that are lighter and more plant-based?

If you have answered yes to any of these questions, then you are lifting your energetic vibration. The planet is decluttering at a rapid rate. You are following suit and are reflecting the energy. The planet requires a higher vibrational space. You also require this. Coming from a higher vibrational space simply means you are able to create a better world for you. If the individual soul can focus on creating their better individual world, then, as a collective, you are able to create a better planet. This is happening now. Focus on your world, your life. If you are destined to create a higher vibrational world from a more public platform, then do not worry as you will be called up. For now, focus on your world and your space.

Begin by making yourself a priority in your life. We have observed this is easier said than done. Many of you are more focused on putting yourself last in an effort to create a more positive life. We say to you, if you continue to focus on those around you, then a more positive life will be elusive. We hear you say, 'I am a parent. My children are my priority and have to be, especially when they are young'. Our answer is this: you are correct that your offspring have needs only parents can provide. It is inherent in your DNA that you ensure your offspring are fed, clean, have shelter, and are nurtured in a loving environment. However, to lose yourself in a parenting role, long after the offspring are independent, can prevent you from experiencing the fullness of you. You can miss the opportunity of experiencing you in many forms, other than the role of a parent/husband/wife/partner.

To give yourself permission to experience activities that make you happy and more content as a person is a wonderful thing to do. It does not make you a neglectful parent/daughter/son/wife/husband unless, of course, you are choosing activities that are harmful to your health, both mentally and physically. But if you partake in experiences that assist you in becoming a happier and steadier person, then this change will be felt by those around you and especially by those you love the most.

Yet We have observed that many of you have lived or are choosing to live a life of servitude to another person. To those who are practising this, We lovingly ask this question, 'Are your own needs and desires less important and less deserving than who you are being of service to?'.

CHAPTER EIGHT: THE BUSINESS OF LIFE

We understand this may take some time to process. You have been conditioned to believe others come before you especially if you are a female. The controlling energy fed this conditioning and helped you believe you are less than the next person. In fact, it sent you people and experiences that reflected this as the law of attraction came into play. The law of *like attracts like* is true. All the beliefs that you hold will be played out in your life. If you do not value yourself, then others will not value you. If you believe you are a servant, you will attract a master. If you feel you are not wealthy, then you will be poor. These limiting beliefs are carried in your energy field that tells the story of who you are. If you want change, We suggest changing your story. This is done by having a positive belief system that will work with the new energy flow rather than against it. You are a powerful expression of the Creator.

With the emergent energy and your divine spark relit, you will be more inclined to look closely at your own feelings and what you truly desire. It will assist you to experience life in a more balanced fashion, and you will nurture yourself. This way you will begin to experience the fullness of you - an amazing being!

You will be able to move beyond your current experience with the power of your intention. We reiterate that never before have you been able to manifest so quickly and easily. All you are required to do is to listen and be aware of the opportunities presented to you that will help you to manifest your intention.

Can you feel the buzz? Can you feel your divine spark jump a little as you read these words? Are you excited? Or are you more thoughtful? Will you leave this book for a little while and experiment a bit to test this theory out or will you read on and make more new discoveries?

CHAPTER NINE

This is the Time

Time.

What is it and does it exist? According to many of you, time is of the utmost importance. It is truly a governing power in your life. You base how productive your day has been according to what you have done in the hours of the day. You are paid hourly. You charge an hourly rate, there is a rush hour, an hourglass, after hours meetings, appointment times, opening times, closing times, time frames, time restrictions, and timetables. The reference to time is extensive and exhaustive.

Do you feel a sense of tiredness creeping over you from reading these words? Are you nodding your head in agreement?

Are you recalling times when you were pressed for time or you may be thinking, 'Oh, this is necessary, because without some sort of structure there would be chaos and anarchy'? From Our observations, there is chaos and anarchy with time structures in place. The chaos is reflected in both your outer world and inner world, and the business of time adds to the busyness of your lives. You may see your outer world as being in a general state of unrest and distrust. This may be how you are feeling internally – unsure of yourself and unsettled. Time constraints add to the burden of this easiness, both on the world stage and in your own personal life.

The controlling energy was very obliging in helping you to be time conscious and time stressed. It loved the busyness of you and constantly aided your need to be purposeful and valid during work times, school times, university times, and family times. It helped you to become these stressed experiences, to identify with them, to remember them with amazing acuity or better yet, to make these experiences even bigger and more dramatic so you would become them. The more stressed experiences you have, the more you became the stress, and the more you identified with the less positive side of things. Can you see how this works?

Now what is very exciting is that the emergent energy encourages a free-flowing life. It is not based on, nor does it encourage, time-based concepts. It allows you to move

CHAPTER NINE: THIS IS THE TIME

through life at your pace and helps you achieve what you desire. All you are encouraged to do is call on it whenever you require its assistance.

For instance, you are in traffic and have 15 minutes to arrive or you will be late. You are nervously thinking of all the worst possibilities that will befall you when you arrive at your destination. Previously, the controlling energy would have eagerly fed this thought pattern. Now, however, there is a different scenario. Your spark has been relit, you are aware of the emergent energy, and you summon it to help. You feel a calm come over you, or suddenly the traffic begins to flow, or you feel a sense of safety and surety that all will be well. It will ensure the situation is taken care of.

The significant difference is the emergent energy is very good at breaking up lower vibrational thought forms that can take hold during moments of stress and fear. The purpose and focus are to create a higher vibrational space for each of you and the planet. All you are encouraged to do is call it forth and allow it to do the job. Endeavour to remove yourself from your expectation of an outcome based on what you are seeing and feeling from a fearful perspective. Let it go. Feel the new energy.

Do you understand now? Let Us briefly summarise.

The controlling energy encouraged more of your fear during times of stress. It was very good at coming up with more fearful outcomes if you were late for work, if you failed an exam, if you were to tell a loved one how you really feel. In fact, it served to amplify the very worst feelings within you, thus stopping you from moving through the situation in a more confident manner. This current higher vibrational energy readily helps you to address the situation in a positive way. It calms and strengthens your being and amplifies the positive feelings that you have within, drawing it forth, and assisting you in receiving a positive outcome.

If you had wished for a constant blissful life, you would not have chosen to reside in human form. Choosing a mortal body means you carry all the baggage that comes with being a mortal. The human form is an amazing experience for growth and learning, and you are meant to navigate the twists and turns this planetary life offers. However, you were meant to navigate life with a more balanced perspective that helps you find far more straight paths than winding ones. What has happened to many of you is that the twists and the turns are far too many and happen far too frequently. As a result, you became lost, and the more lost you felt the more fear-based you became, until you became fear. This fear-based thought form was perfect for the controlling energy. It loved it and amplified it and enveloped you in it more and more until you could not remember ever *not being lost*.

CHAPTER NINE: THIS IS THE TIME

Now, this emergent energy is a guiding light for you to find your way out of the maze. It is so powerful, it can clearly light the way for you and help you to find yourself again. As a mortal, you will encounter the highs and lows of life. This is your humanity and free will. No being has the power to remove this aspect from you whilst you are human. The wonderful news is that the emergent energy will help you create a higher way of living for yourself and others around you. You will be more content.

We encourage you to feel that you are time rich rather than time poor. By switching to this train of thought, you will find that you will arrive at your destination on time, complete that task, finish that assignment. As you feel time rich, your physical body will not feel as pressured but have more energy. We have observed that an energetic physical body is a great advantage to your everyday life.

How are you feeling at this point? Are you feeling hopeful? Are you feeling more positive? If so, then this is a good thing, and you may wish to read on. If you have little doubts creep into your mind at the notion that you could be happier by drawing forth the energy, then it may be time for you to put down the book and allow the words to integrate a bit more. Whatever you choose will be the best decision for you.

CHAPTER TEN

Energy

Welcome back again. How are you feeling? Did you plunge right back into this book or did you place it aside for a few days, few weeks, or even months?

Back to the emergent energy. We have spoken to you about the concept of time and how it can be very restrictive and influential in your day-to-day life. Routine and structure have much importance to many of you as this is how you get the job done, juggle family, fit in exercise, and social outings. This is a helpful concept if used in a balanced way. What is not helpful is when you become obsessed with trying to fit everything into a time frame, and when this does not happen,

CHAPTER TEN: ENERGY

a state of unrest and panic may be felt. We have noticed you can almost become dependent on being busy, and when you find free time (what does this really mean anyway), you fill it up with busyness. You are conditioned to believe that busyness is productive, and you seek to fill your spare time with activities that reflect this. You may clean out a cupboard, clean the car, wash the dog, cut the lawn, sweep the floor, or the big one, amuse yourself with technology for a while.

You may be thinking that using technology is a relaxing thing. You are not activating anything. You are sitting down and taking your mind off a certain problem. You are giving your brain a rest. We say to you, if you continue to fill in your free time with electronics, then you are being busy. Your mind is busy. It is being stimulated by outside programs and influences that seep into your being. You are being affected by external stimuli designed to influence the brain in such a manner that there is no off button for it. There is not even a pause button. There is a constant whirring of information encircling your brain and interfering with your own unique frequency. The controlling energy loved this. It encouraged you to seek out that which provides constant stimulus and distraction. It loved helping you feel more disconnected from your own frequency pattern. It was very powerful in helping you fill in time with the perception of relaxation, when, in fact, it was the complete opposite.

The emergent energy encourages you to feel in a more relaxed state of being. You will easily manage to get the children to cricket practice, get that paper handed in, complete the proposal, organise that meeting, get to the airport on time, prepare dinner, and organise the week. You will find you will be less drawn to electronics but would rather do other activities that promote the more creative side of you. What is even more important is the new energy will provide many opportunities to connect with Spirit. This is a very exciting thing, and one We will explore later.

Once again, We ask, how are you feeling?

Perhaps you may be thinking (not feeling) that some of what you are reading is very similar to other books you have read, and this is old stuff retold again. We say that, yes – you are right. The concepts are the same, however, the emphasis is that these concepts can be readily put into action more easily than ever before. Why? Because this emergent energy encourages you to do just this. It provides more of a direct path to your destination and will steer you away from all the twists and turns you previously encountered. This is the difference. This is the truth. This is the way to a happier mortal life until you reach the end of the journey… at least in this lifetime.

CHAPTER ELEVEN

The Birthing of the Planet

$\mathcal{L}$et Us now discuss how your planet came into existence. But first, We ask you, have you felt less inclined to amuse the brain with flickering lights, distorted sounds, and the endless need to win against an inanimate object? Have you tried to disengage from stressful situations and conversations that seem to go around and around with no resolution in sight? Are you beginning to see this world from a new perspective and doubt all that is being broadcast to you? Are you coming up with more questions about the world and its workings and perhaps seeing that many things do not make sense?

If you are, then you are beginning to become aware of who you truly are. You are a sentient being that comes from the same Source energy as Us. We are, in fact, one and the same. It is just that you are operating in a different frequency on a planet that *was* vibrating at quite a low frequency. Note that We use the words *was* vibrating. This is significant as, currently, the planet and you are beginning to vibrate at a higher frequency level.

This has all come about due to the fact that Source has decreed that this planet be freed from the lower vibrational forces that have occupied and taken hold of it for many thousands of years. Yes, the energy of the planet has been tampered with to create an environment and a life that has enslaved you by helping you feel disconnected from Source and yourself. You chose to experience this planet for a myriad of reasons, but the BIG reason was that you wanted to break up the controlling energy and to bring light to this world. Every time you lived on this planet, and, for many of you reading this book it has been hundreds if not thousands of times, your choice was to bring light to this world. Your choice was to evolve and become a better version of yourself. Many of you chose horrendous ways to allow your light to shine. You were subjected to torture, poverty, abuse in all

CHAPTER ELEVEN: THE BIRTHING OF THE PLANET

forms, slavery, and persecution. Many times, you had very sad existences upon this planet, yet still you chose to come back, again and again. Such is your dedication to the Light.

The controlling energy loved seeing you suffer. It aided you in your suffering. It even encouraged other souls to increase your suffering. It entrapped you. It fed freely from your feelings of powerlessness. It was particularly happy when you railed against God or any energy you felt gave you peace and strength. It encouraged you to feel isolated, let down and unsupported, for these feelings are created from a place of fear and disconnection. It fed the reality that you began to create for yourself until you became lost in it and you became conditioned.

Conditioning. How do you feel when you read this word? Does it spark an understanding or a sense of familiarity? Do you have a little shudder in your being when you feel the power of this word and how it was used for thousands of years to help you feel powerless and at the mercy of others?

You have been conditioned innumerable times as you lived here on Earth. Were you aware that this planet was birthed with the Mother Energy and came into existence with the exhale of Source? This was the same for your solar system, however, Earth was, and is, of special significance.

When this planet was born many beings from different dimensions visited it and felt the energy of the Mother. It was unlike anything they had experienced, and thus it helped them to spiritually evolve. This planet was one of Source's finest creation and was many times larger than it is now.

It became smaller through the crashing of a wayward planet over 500,000 years ago. Suffice to say that, after this collision, Earth has never been the same. We will talk more of this at another time, but, for now, allow these words to sink into your consciousness to help you prepare for some deeper information to come. If you feel inclined, We encourage you to further research your planet's collision when you are ready.

For thousands of years, Earth was simply energy. It did not have rivers or lakes, nor mountain ranges, nor an ecosystem. It simply emanated an energy and many beings were drawn to this frequency. As the Mother Energy settled, She began to create for herself. This was when the rivers, lakes, oceans, and land masses came into being. You are probably aware that the land formations were very different to what they are now. This is because energy moves and vibrates. Energy naturally flows. The Mother Energy then opened her heart to the beings that visited her and invited them to have an existence upon Her creation. And so, many different beings from many different universes and dimensions took

CHAPTER ELEVEN: THE BIRTHING OF THE PLANET

up residence. The original inhabitants were not motivated to create chaos or wreak havoc upon the planet. Instead, they learnt about the Mother energy and lived in peace upon Her.

These beings used the natural resources that the Earth Mother provided. There was no need for fire for the weather was temperate, and at this time there was no snow or ice. It was an idyllic environment. When a being had enough of living in this frequency, a portal opened, and it returned to where it came from to report and give testimony of its experience. In fact, all beings that co-created and learnt from the Mother became imbued with the Mother's energy, thus lifting their vibrational frequency to another level. You can see why your planet attracted much interest from many life forms whose motives were to elevate their consciousness with love and reverence.

Thus, many beings co-created with the Earth. With the Earth Mother's permission, they brought forth species of flowers, trees, crystals, rocks, minerals, and even small animals and fish. Everything was balanced and in perfect harmony. As Earth evolved, so did the Earth Mother. She yearns to return to Source. To do so, as with all beings, there must be an evolution of self.

After the altering of the planet when She broke apart, part of Earth became the asteroid belt currently located between Mars and Jupiter. With the breaking of her body, She (who became known as Gaia) was altered and vulnerable. It was at this point that the darker forces roaming the skies and the universes settled here, and then began the years of tyranny and enslavement, creating a planet of imbalance and deception.

As humankind populated the planet and the Earth became in crises, the clarion-call sounded throughout the multiverse to assist Earth in its plight. However, We and others like Us were restricted as to how much We could help for We could not interfere with your free will. All We could do was watch and wait and endeavour to protect Earth from being tormented by other harmful energies that wanted to further cause planetary destruction.

We would like to offer this analogy of Earth's battle: if you can imagine yourself being caught in a net so strong that the more you struggle to become free, the tighter the net becomes. This aptly describes humans and Gaia trying to release themselves from the controlling energy. The dark net is so strong rescuers cannot cut through it with the sharpest and most powerful tool available to them. In fact, to do so would be to possibly damage or hurt you in the process. That is not feasible. What is needed is for you, who is trapped in the net, to find a weakness from within. Some sort of point that, bit by bit, you could wear down until it becomes so weak there is an opening for rescuers to use their resources

CHAPTER ELEVEN: THE BIRTHING OF THE PLANET

to cut you free with minimal damage. As you struggle to free yourself, help is always at hand, trying to give you sustaining nourishment so that you do not falter.

This is exactly what has happened over these thousands of years. Light Beings from every universe have heeded the call for help and have watched the planet struggle while looking for ways to make their way in. You have incarnated, again and again, to create the light and find a way for the Earth to become free. But the darker energy was so strong that once you were here it was difficult for you to remember who you are and why you came. You were poisoned at every level to keep you in ignorance and fear, and you became conditioned and, therefore, powerless.

We have watched this unfold and have endeavoured to pour as much of Our enlightened energy into each soul and the planet. Some has managed to make its way through but very little, akin to pouring a drop of water every day on a plant exposed to incessant heat. The water drop was just enough to sustain it but did not help it to flourish and grow in strength so it could find its own water using its root system.

Now, the time has come where there are enough enlightened souls upon the planet that have broken free of the illusion and deception that finally We are able to make Our way in and help you at a deeper and more powerful level. Awakened souls lift their own frequency and that of the Earth's, and this creates the opportunity for change. Change is upon you NOW! Change will occur, the distinguishing factor is whether you want more of the same for the next 26,000 years or you desire a more fair, balanced, and wholesome planet. We say to you that the transformative years are taking place now, more specifically from 2013 to 2027 earth years. If you truly desire a better world, then the key is to wake up and take notice of what is going on around you and stand steadfast in your power.

Can you feel this perceptible change of energy? Can you feel the truth in these words, and do you find your spirit lifting? If you do, then this is a very good thing. It means that you are shedding your conditioning and opening yourself up to the truth of who, and what, you are. Alternatively, if you are feeling confused and not quite sure about the last entry, then it may be a good time to put down the book and leave it for another day.

We also encourage you to seek out information, to research Earth's breaking apart thousands of years ago, to make discoveries for yourself. In this instance, the efficiency in finding information using your technology is a gift. Use it. Question. Discover. Discuss. Remember.

You are always welcome to invite Us to partake in any discussion. We are here to assist and help you shift beyond your current circumstance. Please make use of Us!

CHAPTER TWELVE

You are the New Energy

If you put down this book for a while, welcome back. Let Us continue.

We have spoken about the birthing of this planet and then the corruption that took place thousands of years ago. We have explained that it is now time for the birthing of the new energy and that your divine spark has been relit in order for you to become part of this energy. We have said that, by embracing the emergent energy, you have the opportunity to create a much happier version of yourself. We have said all this. Do you agree?

What We have not said is how do you know you have truly become part of this energy, and what may happen when you fully understand this.

You will know when you have become part of this energy as you will begin to *feel* more rather than think about the world. In fact, you will be guided more on how you feel about any experience, and you will begin to automatically ask yourself, 'How does this feel to me?'. Notice the 'me' reference in this sentence. In the past, the question may have been, 'How will he/she react if I said/did this?' Do you see the difference? You were more focused on the reaction of the other party rather than how you felt about the situation.

We have found that many times your thought processes centre on some type of conforming on your part. For example, you may have thought, 'I dare not wear this colour as my partner does not like it on me'. Well, We say, 'Do you feel this colour looks good on you, and do you feel happy wearing it?'

When you are in alignment with yourself, you will always choose the very best outcome for you. You will dress appropriately, you will talk appropriately, you will do business appropriately, you will study appropriately.

CHAPTER TWELVE: YOU ARE THE NEW ENERGY

Do you understand now? When you become part of this emergent energy, you are automatically in alignment with yourself. You automatically feel when something is amiss with what you are doing. You will put a top or pair of pants on, and then stand in the mirror and automatically know if the colour suits you or not. You will base this decision on how you feel about the colour rather than how someone else feels about it. Do you understand the difference?

This is a very simple example, but it can be applied to all activities in your life including the very big one that causes many of you much pain and anguish: relationships. The relationships with your lover, mother, father, brother, sister, aunt, uncle have caused much heartache and sorrow for you. This is because many times you have been focused on the reaction and expectations of the other person. In many cases, you were programmed to completely disregard your feelings towards the relationship and instead focus on the feelings of the other person. Much of your energy was spent on ensuring the other person was kept happy. This could be anything from making sure there were cooked meals, a spotless house, or less interaction with friends to listening to their music, only socialising with their friends, becoming quiet when they were angry, and, the big one, accepting abuse from them.

Know that any deliberate physical, mental, or emotional trauma that one soul inflicts on another is regarded as soul-destroying by all enlightened beings. On your planet, this attracts thousands of earth years in the karmic cycle, and, yet, We see this continually play out with very little thought to the consequences that enslaved Earth's inhabitants. Know also that the controlling energy very much fed these angry emotions making it easier for vengeful and harmful thought patterns to be carried out. This is another reason why the clearing of karmic debt and soul contracts, is so very necessary in your present time. Never before have humans had the opportunity to do so, with such ease. To "wipe the slate" clean is very much encouraged by Us.

We have observed that many of you were intent on trying to please another in order for this person to like and/or accept you. Many of you twisted yourself inside out to recreate a version of yourself that was more pleasing to them. Now We say that, as you become part of this new energy, you will recreate a version of yourself that is more pleasing to *you*.

You will begin to experience your own personal power and become aware of your own unique frequency. This awareness will lead you on the road to freedom. The emergent energy encourages this behaviour. It literally seeks out the realness of you and assists you in developing and becoming your truth. More importantly, it holds you

CHAPTER TWELVE: YOU ARE THE NEW ENERGY

steadfast in your own ability. It will help you move beyond situations that previously imprisoned you because you have the strong intention to do so.

The emergent energy resonates very strongly with your highest good intention. It will assist you in leaving behind controlling relationships, jobs, and anything that previously enabled you to feel small and powerless. It will do this by suggestions, sending people to aid you, helping you find your voice to express how you feel, keeping you safe, giving you the courage and the means to leave the experience. In all manner of ways, it will assist you. All you are encouraged to do is to act on this feeling.

We have said that you have free will. While you are in human form and on this planet, your free will shall influence what you want for yourself and even how you go about it. The difference is that your free will in the new energy will be very much motivated by the desire to help you find happiness that, in turn, can create happiness for those around you. The controlling energy encouraged your free will to be more selfish in its intention and, in fact, tried to mislead you away from happiness and more towards discontent.

Now, your free will decision-making shall come from a place of joy rather than fear. You will find that you are less fearful of the consequences of leaving a relationship, job, career, study, or home. You will feel the courage and certainty within you that all will be well. You are driven by your desire to find happiness for yourself, for, by doing so, you will find happiness within others around you.

How are you feeling about these words? Are you encouraged to try, or are you feeling a bit doubtful about how easy this sounds? We understand you are used to things being a bit of an effort. Indeed, the controlling energy was an expert at helping you expend energy on anything that remotely led to freedom. The exhaustion from trying to change experiences in your life was very beneficial in keeping you locked in powerlessness.

We say to you: monitor your breath. Be aware of it. It is one of the greatest tools at your disposal and is capable of much more than keeping you oxygenated and nourished. Your breath activates your spark and flows the energy around your body and deep into your cells. Breathe. In times of stress, just breathe and allow the emergent energy to take hold of you and lift you above the stress.

CHAPTER THIRTEEN

You are Renewed

You are renewed. What does this mean? What do you feel it means?

From Our viewpoint, this means you are standing at the threshold of a whole new existence. An existence that is based on you creating a happier life for you, your loved ones, and the planet. This comes from the reigniting of the divine spark, which allows you to become the new energy flowing into the Earth. This emergent energy cannot be corrupted or tampered with. It is a pure high vibrational and pulsating force of Light. It carries the essences of many Light Beings, and, most of all, it contains the Source Light and the Mother Energy.

This means that you are renewed, and this planet is renewed. Great plans have been made to help this planet heal and rebuild in ways that will truly astound you. To say that there is a grand plan on a massive scale is a huge understatement. The plan has come from Source, and Source can be many things at once and can orchestrate the perceived impossible to happen. Impossibility is not Source. Source is all things possible. We encourage you to understand this a little bit better in order for you to comprehend what will take place very soon.

CHAPTER THIRTEEN: YOU ARE RENEWED

Know that as your divine spark has been relit, and so has the Earth Mother's. She is ascending. You may have read this before in other books or heard it from other people. You may have known this for a long time, so this is not news to you. It is true. This planet has been preparing to ascend for many decades, and now the countdown is truly on.

We hear you say. 'Well, this has been said for many years, so why should I believe it now?'

We say to you: look at the world around you. Really look at it. Can you see and feel the chaos that is surrounding you? Do you hear the media cover such sad stories of death, war, and destruction? Do you see Governments increasing their entitlements and decreasing yours? Do you feel the sense of despair that is pervading most souls on the planet, despite their every attempt to remain centred and balanced? Do you see no relief or an end in sight to this madness?

If you have answered yes to most of the above, then be assured that the change is coming. Be assured that the light is strong in its power to change and to bring balance back to the Earth and its inhabitants. The controlling lower vibrational energy that has taken command of this planet is hanging on for grim life. We use the word *life* deliberately. The lower frequencies are desperate to survive and maintain power, and, to do so, they are throwing everything at everyone. This is how you know the time is near. It is the very reason that there is so much chaos and confusion, for there is much of the opposite that is occurring at the same time.

There is a weeding out of the lower frequencies, and a new grid of light is being prepared to cover the planet. The corrupted energy net that was covering the planet has become tattered and torn, and very vulnerable in some spots. As a result, the new energy is forming and covering the vast majority of the planet and is now focussing on fusing its energy into you to bring about change.

Can you feel your divine spark jump in your chest at these words? Can you feel the stir of excitement and a sense of knowing that the time for change is almost here? Does this resonate more truly within you now? Does it not seem such a faraway thing?

The planet is being renewed. It is awash with higher frequencies while, at the same time, it is trying to shake off the invaders that are causing it harm much like an animal trying to rid itself of fleas after a nice wash and application of a repellent.

This new energy repels all energy that is created for darkness and ill intent. Its sole purpose is to cleanse and clear all that is not in resonance with it. It literally stirs

CHAPTER THIRTEEN: YOU ARE RENEWED

and shakes things up so much that you can see and feel the fleas exiting their host.

This is happening at a planetary level and at an individual level. With your divine spark being relit, you will feel that you have less tolerance for all things that are not in resonance with you. You will be greatly motivated to bring about changes to bring in that resonance. It cannot be otherwise.

Can you feel the truth in these words? Are you not at this very minute questioning and wondering about situations in your own life that can be improved? Can you no longer push these thoughts away from you to look at later?

CHAPTER FOURTEEN

The Power of Intention

'How do I bring about these changes?', you may be asking.

This is a very good question, and We have a very simple answer - *you intend for change to happen*. We understand that you may have heard and read of this before. We know you have been inundated with the word *intend*. We also know you may have tried to do this but very little has happened to bring about the change that you have asked for.

We say again to you that this time is very different. The current energy helps bring in positive change. Note that We say,

CHAPTER FOURTEEN: THE POWER OF INTENTION

positive change. Remember that this energy cannot be tampered with or corrupted. Even your own free will choices will have a hard time bringing energy into your life that can assist you in being less than you are. This is because you are becoming free from the conditioning that has pervaded your life to date. You have been conditioned to create from fear. Most of all, the past energy was effective in blocking your intention to manifest changes that could lift your vibration and regain your power.

In the past, you could see that you needed to bring about change and create a happier life for yourself. You endeavoured to do this by being mindful of the way you perceived experiences, and you were careful with your word choices and mind thoughts. This you tried very hard to do, and when small positive changes manifested, you felt you had succeeded, and you became happier with your version of life.

What We have noticed is that many of you settled for the smallest of positive changes, and you perceived that this was good enough. Many of you settled for less than what you truly felt you deserved and wanted. Many of you thought, 'This is as good as it gets' and decided it was best not to strive or desire anything more.

Say, for example, you are in a relationship that does not satisfy you. You are aware of the power of intention, and so you intend for the relationship to become more satisfying for you. After a while of diligent intention, you notice that your partner begins to smile a bit more and is less moody. You are happy with this result. You think that your intention has worked, you have manifested a more satisfying relationship and are feeling better. This is a good thing, but it has only worked to a point. Your partner is still jealous of you going out with friends and does not completely trust you. Yet you are willing to settle for the smallest of positive change, so you think that this shift in your partner is good enough. Oh, you may have wanted her to trust you more, but then again, is it really unreasonable for her to ask where you are going and to make sure you are alright, and to insist that socialising with other people will take away time with each other?

So, you make excuses for why you should settle for your partner smiling more and being less grumpy when what you truly wanted was for her to trust and not be so possessive of you. The controlling energy encouraged you to settle for the smallest of positive change and supported the excuses you made for your partner's trust issues. It encouraged you to stay in an experience that was less than what you truly wanted.

The emergent energy encourages you to settle for so much more. It will align your intention to bring about the most positive change you desire and, most of all, it discourages you from settling for anything less. So, you will find that you will not settle for a more smiley and less grumpy partner that still insists on monitoring your every move. The new energy will help you

CHAPTER FOURTEEN: THE POWER OF INTENTION

bring about a change in that relationship that may involve you leaving it behind or propelling your partner forward in seeking changes in himself/herself that will benefit the both of you.

Do you understand Our words? Your intention is most important. It is the catalyst for change in your life. Unlike before, you will not settle for less because your divine spark has been relit, and you have the innate desire to keep creating a positive life for yourself. The energy will bring about the means to do so. All you are encouraged to do is to keep the intention and to follow the signposts that lead you up the path to a happier state of being.

Is this not exciting? Can you feel yourself smiling at this thought? Can you feel yourself thinking, 'Is this for real?'. Can it be now? Can it be so easy?

Indeed, the time has come. You are in the creative flow of life. You are part of the new emergent energy. Your unique frequency and the higher vibrational energy can bring happiness and, most of all, sustain happiness whilst you are in human form. You will feel the ebb and flow of the energy, and you will experience sadness and pain at times for you are human. What you will not do is become the sad experience or stay in the sad experience because this is not your desire. You are a powerful being, a wonderful experience of both spiritual and human, and We are looking forward to assisting you to grow and begin a brand-new world.

CHAPTER FIFTEEN

Positive Changes

Perhaps, by now, you have an understanding that the past and the current world you are experiencing has, in fact, been controlled and tampered with. It has been led away from the prime intention of the original creation.

The original intention was for this planet to be a very positive and happy experience for all beings who chose to come here. The planet was birthed by Source as a divine expression of the feminine energy, which was the first of its kind to come into being. Thus, it attracted the attention of many beings from many different dimensions and galaxies. Some chose to embrace this wondrous experience,

CHAPTER FIFTEEN: POSITIVE CHANGES

some chose to acknowledge the uniqueness of it and then returned to their chosen dimension, whilst others chose to try and control this planet and started a form of experimentation. The planet went into lockdown, and while many beings tried valiantly to halt and intercept the flow of corruption, they could not. To do so would have put the planet and her inhabitants at risk, and this was not an option. All expressions of Source are honoured, even the lowest vibrational form of experience. This is the decree of the Creator, and all beings of high vibration honour this.

We hear you say, 'Well, this does not bode well for us. It could have saved lifetimes of misery if Spirit would have intercepted sooner. Should not the Creator have done something about this earlier?'

Our answer is one of deepness and simplicity: Source will not destroy or turn inwards upon itself. It will always seek divinity and high vibration. Such is the love it holds, Source will send other expressions of itself to help the lower expressions to remember who they are. Source's core principle is to allow its own expression to create freely until that aspect of itself has created all it wants to create, and it returns to itself.

Does this sound a bit confusing to you? Read the last paragraph again, and feel your divine spark react in understanding.

You, who are reading or listening to this book, are a unique expression of Source. Your divine spark is an expression of Source - it is your true identity. Your human form and brain are an extension of that expression. It is a form that allows you to create whatever you choose to create. Your human form is expertly designed as Source created the form, and Source is an expert at designing and creating.

What has happened is that your form has been tampered with and corrupted so that you are trying to create from fear and, in many cases, from what people think you should be. You endeavour to live up to their expectation of you, rather than you living as your true expression. You have been inundated by thought forms that indoctrinate you into believing what you should look like, how you should act, what you should have, where you should work, what religion you should practice, and what government dictates. You have been held in a limiting belief system that seeks to assist you in being less than you are.

As a result, many of you have attracted situations that have led to sadness, fear, and a general unwellness. This can be reflected in your personal, family and work relationships, not to mention your own relationship with self! Your human body, which was designed to be robust and have longevity, has become weakened and vulnerable,

CHAPTER FIFTEEN: POSITIVE CHANGES

and many have transitioned into a painful and scared state of being. This was never the intention for the planet.

As We mentioned before, beings who chose to inhabit this planet simply stepped into a portal and returned to where they came. There was no death as you know it. There was no suffering. There was no injury. There was no destruction of the planet or its inhabitants. All that was intentioned was for this planet to be experienced in all its forms. To feel the energy and how the Earth Mother created, and what She created. All that was intentioned was for those that lived here to feel the energy and co-create with Her. Not to co-create against Her. Do you understand this?

Those inhabitants who lovingly and consciously created with Gaia used Her creations to further create. Thus, crystals came into being. Structures of incredible geometry and precision were used to capture the movement of the stars and the planets and to serve as beacons of energy and portals to other dimensions. Everything was in harmony. Everything was balanced. Everything was divine. Everything was perfect.

Source and Gaia have now decreed that She return to Her original state of being. To do this, it is necessary for the lower vibrational energy to leave and a higher level of consciousness to take its place. This has been the plan for many, many years, and now this plan is coming to fruition.

As We have previously stated, you can see the outworking of many previous belief systems that were set in place to control and manipulate Earth's inhabitants. There is general unrest all around the globe as wars are fought to claim territory, resources, and people. Even those countries who do not wish to feel the effect of world matters are no longer able to sit by and watch idly while events unfold. All are being called to begin the process of letting go of the old and bringing in the new world.

This is a coming of a new era. There are bringers of light and inventions that are managing to make their way into this magnificent planet. There is a whole new infrastructure that is being set up that will affect every human and non-human on this Earth. We use this word non-human deliberately, and We will briefly touch on this subject before We proceed.

You have been sharing your planet with beings that do not carry your particular form of DNA structure. Your DNA structure is primitive and not fully functional. It has even been referred to as containing junk DNA. It is, in fact, not junk, but instead contains data that allows you to be very much more than you currently resemble physically, mentally, emotionally and spiritually. We say to you that much of your DNA has been switched off deliberately to keep you from discovering who you really are.

CHAPTER FIFTEEN: POSITIVE CHANGES

Because your DNA is working at only minimal capacity, it was quite apparent that in order to bring enlightenment to this planet and the human civilisation, then beings from other universes would need to integrate amongst the population to help shift the mass-energy consciousness. Their very presence, with their fuller genetic DNA working, has helped ignite the creative minds of many of your famous people, particularly in the field of music. Hence, some compositions that appeared in the 1800s contained notes of a subliminal high frequency that reverberated within the pineal gland and was sorely needed during the Dark Ages, aptly named, as it was a period of intense trauma.

There has always been the presence of Extra Terrestrials (to use your human term) on your planet. Now, many of these beings are working with you, but, as you may understand, there are also beings that actively work at keeping you dormant and stagnant.

Souls who have chosen to undertake a more public platform are carefully being positioned to help bring about the change. These very enlightened beings are, at this very moment, downloading information that will facilitate a new way of living. These humans are present in countries across the world and are taking their place in parliaments, councils, corporations, financial institutions, medical establishments, schools, and all places that are in dire need of restructuring and the implementation of new energy.

You, who have accessed this book, may feel the tug of understanding and desire to create change. You may be currently active in some of the aforementioned places and may already receive nuggets of information or feelings of how to bring about the necessary changes. We say to you that you are well on your way to achieving this.

To those who are struggling in their workplace and wondering why you are there, then the answer is this: you are the bringer of change. You have chosen to become part of the change in systems that are in most need of this change. We mainly refer to the health and educational systems that have been neglected. This is where the focus of the energy corruption has been. The structure and setup of these two systems have instead created sickness and ignorance. Can you feel the truth of this statement? Are you not already seeing the effects of this in the world around you?

We encourage you not to lose hope or become bogged down in the feelings of despair and hopelessness that you may feel in your workplace. Know that, with the relighting of your divine spark, you can be now less affected by the energy around you, and the feelings of frustration and

CHAPTER FIFTEEN: POSITIVE CHANGES

hopelessness will lessen. As these feelings lessen, you will find you are filled with more hope and enthusiasm, and you will then have the ability to light the divine spark in others around you.

In your place of work, which is not in alignment with its true state of being, a change is able to take place by bringing in the emergent energy. One way this can be done is by your ability to light the divine spark of souls in your place of work, which in turn will allow that soul to be more in alignment with the new energy on the planet. As more and more souls in the workplace are in alignment with the new energy, the necessary changes can be made. The new energy cannot tolerate anything that is less than what it is.

This will happen in other areas of your life including family and friends. You may find that you will enjoy the company of different people. Those that you previously spent time with may move away from you. This is the Law of Attraction at work the understanding that like attracts like. As your energy vibration shifts, people and experiences that you previously enjoyed may not hold the same attraction to you. You may innately seek the company of others that are more aware. If you experience this, please do not be alarmed. This is part of the shift, and it will occur naturally.

Now may be a good time to put down the book and allow this concept to flow through your body. We especially encourage those of you who are finding it challenging working in an environment that is suffering under the influence of ego-driven decisions to take a while to absorb this. We would encourage you to put Our words to the test, to see for yourself; to consciously call on your divine spark to keep you balanced at all times, and to assist in being less affected by the energy around you. We support you to consciously ask to help relight the divine spark in your workmates. Do this. Test it out. Why not?

We also encourage you to research Our information regarding your DNA structure, and, in particular, consider why would your genetic material contain the so-called 'junk'? Why would Source create such a wondrous marvel as your human body but not allow it to express the fullness of what it is capable of? Why would Source switch off parts of the genetic structure of Its creation? We offer these questions to open your mind and increase your level of awareness.

This may be the perfect time for you to record how you are feeling, to take note of any changes that have occurred or any light bulb moments you have felt. Perhaps write down questions of your own that you are seeking answers to.

CHAPTER FIFTEEN: POSITIVE CHANGES

The following two pages are left blank for you to put pen to paper. Once again, if you do not feel any inclination to write, then this is fine, but We say to you again: this is an energy book. By choosing to record snippets of insights, you are contributing to this book and adding your energy to it. You are co-creating something wonderful with Us. This is a marvellous and very powerful thing to do.

If you are listening to this book, now may be the time to tell of the insights you have had or to also write information down. Understand that, as you have continued to read up to this point, this book is truly yours. The likelihood of you giving away this book to another person and them seeing what you have written is unlikely, so We invite you to record freely. You will marvel at how far you have come!

CHAPTER FIFTEEN: POSITIVE CHANGES

CHAPTER SIXTEEN

The Importance of Choice

In the last chapter, We touched on how to change the energy of the workplace. It can be accomplished by your ability to reignite the divine spark within your colleagues. This can facilitate the newer energy to have greater access to the workplace to bring about the necessary changes to create a better and happier work environment. This also applies to your everyday life as well.

Now that your divine spark has been relit, you are able to live a more authentic and freer state of being than has

CHAPTER SIXTEEN: THE IMPORTANCE OF CHOICE

been possible in aeons of time. We have said that you still have free choice that cannot be removed whilst you are in human form, and the emergent energy is driven by its desire to bring about more positive changes in your lives. It cannot be corrupted or tampered with, and it will always serve to be in alignment with your highest intention to create a happier state of being.

We would like to bring forth the understanding of choice to you now. The majority, or all of your life, has been based upon choice.

You may have read that each of you chose your birth parents and the environment in which you were born. You decreed this before you reincarnated here. In fact, the very first choice you made was to come back to this planet! Many of you have reincarnated on Earth again and again. Oh, there may have been rest intervals between each life. However, many of you desired to reincarnate very soon once you transitioned. This was motivated by your desire to bring light to a planet bathed in darkness.

Another reason that may be news to you is that your very soul, the divine essence of you, could not transition freely. You were a slave of the controlling energy that manipulated and coerced your free will choices to such an extent that you could not leave the planet readily. You managed to accumulate so much karma through desperate choices you made as a human that you were forced to reincarnate numerous times. Thus, your soul came back again and again. When you did reincarnate, you still experienced a disconnection from self and accrued karma and soul contracts, and the cycle was repeated. The strength of the controlling energy was enormous, and its ability to help you forget who you are was very powerful.

During the last thousand years or so, many of you managed to remember that you are a divine being and part of Source. You connected with yourself and began to move away from the conditioning that pervaded the planet. You managed to lift your vibrational frequency enough to allow you to dissolve accrued karma and, more importantly, not to add to the karma or soul contracts you previously owned. This is very important for you to understand. The merest shift of your vibrational frequency during your human lifetime is enough to create a change and stop the karmic wheel, thus helping you transition freely.

Yes! You are creating an opportunity for you to shift karmic debt, release soul contracts and be assured of a clean transitioning from this planet. This is the greatest gift you can offer yourself. Do not underestimate this power. We say to you, the more enlightened you become in your *Now* moment the more joy you will experience in your lives.

CHAPTER SIXTEEN: THE IMPORTANCE OF CHOICE

Let Us discuss further the controlling energy. This energy was very clear and very strong. It was the complete opposite of the energy that is experienced by Us that reside in very high vibrational frequencies. Once you became a higher vibrational soul, you automatically sought to bring this frequency to the planet, and hence the many incarnations you may have experienced. You, as an expression of the Creator, desired to bring more light to a planet that was floundering in the darkness. Does this feel true to you? Do you feel that you have been here many times? Is there an innate knowing that you are an old soul on this planet? Even now, are you motivated to bring forth a positive change to your world? Do you feel you are a Lightworker?

As a higher evolved soul, your intention was to anchor as much light energy as possible to the planet and to assist in the freeing of Gaia. Do you recall that earlier We spoke of the plan to free the planet from the net of corrupted energy that encircled it? Do you recall that higher vibrational beings were seeking ways of severing the net from the outside in so that We could assist in freeing you but were unable? We had to wait until the net became weak in some points and, in order for such a weakness to occur, the vulnerability had to come from the inside out. Your soul choice was to anchor a higher consciousness that would bring about weaknesses in the net. All of you tried. All of you endeavoured, at some stage, to hold this frequency, despite the obstacles and twists and turns you came up against. When you did not succeed at doing this to your intended level, you chose to reincarnate swiftly and numerous times to bring about change. Even though you forgot who you were when you incarnated here, there was, at some level, a desire and intention to behave more lovingly and respectful towards others. This resulted in minimal karma and soul contracts accrued. Do you understand this truth?

The reason why you could not bring about your soul intention was that, as soon as you incarnated, you forgot who you really are. This state of non-remembrance stayed with you during that particular lifetime on the planet. This is simply because the corruptive energy was so powerful it created the veil of illusion. Its aim was to keep you powerless. It actively worked at keeping you in the dark. It presented you with countless opportunities for you to make choices based on fear rather than on your own knowing or your own intuition. It created a world of fear-based thoughts and madness and encouraged you to be part of it. If at some point, you chose to step away from the madness, there were consequences. You were labelled as many things depending on which century you lived: *witch*, *warlock*, *mentally unstable*,

CHAPTER SIXTEEN: THE IMPORTANCE OF CHOICE

mad, loser, weird, rebellious, selfish, black sheep, conspirator, traitor. Many times you suffered for your choice, which was based on the desire for freedom, and many of you died after much suffering. This meant that, when you reincarnated again, you endeavoured once more to bring light and freedom to the planet.

You may be aware of such views of *karma, past lives, soul groups*, and *life lessons*. We say to you that this was indeed the case, and this planet was a wonderful opportunity to advance and accelerate your soul growth. What We also say to you is that much of this was also orchestrated by the corruptive energy that had power to manipulate you at a soul level.

Now may be the time to take a few breaths and clear your mind. For what We are about to impart will require a bit of a mind shift for you. It is a concept you may not be familiar with and, even as you read Our words, you may experience a sense of disbelief and doubt. We reassure you that these feelings are quite alright to experience. It is part of the process of shifting your energy vibration. As We have stated, this is an energy book and every word will have some effect on your energetic system. You will be affected in some way. How much you are affected depends on your free will choice, and We reverently acknowledge this aspect of you.

It is true that this planet served as a wonderful opportunity for a soul's growth. Before each reincarnation, you decided what you wanted to experience and who you wanted each experience with. You may have known that some of the hardest and most painful experiences were the catalyst for huge soul growth. You have been led to believe that you needed to endure many unpleasant experiences in order for you to become a more advanced soul. Those souls that caused these sad experiences were, in fact, Our greatest teachers. Does this sound familiar to you? When you look back on your present life, can you see how past experiences with various people helped shape who you are today?

Do you look back at your current life and feel that you resonate with more painful life situations? Do you more easily recall feelings of sadness, pain, anger, betrayal, and rejection? Do you feel these negative feelings were the greatest catalysts for your evolution into who you are today? Do you resonate more with these experiences?

We would think that many of you easily recall painful past memories. Very few of you first recalled the happier and fun times you have had. These happier times may never have entered your consciousness as a soul growth experience. Many of you may not recall the energies of both people and animals who assisted you on a happier level. You may not have considered them as part of your

CHAPTER SIXTEEN: THE IMPORTANCE OF CHOICE

journey or felt that they have had less of an impact on who you are today. Why is this so?

This is because the corruptive energy has conditioned you to believe that the evolution of your soul is mainly dependent on living a more painful existence and that this is the only way you can advance on a more spiritual level. Along the way, you have accrued and dispensed karma and soul contracts which meant that each reincarnation you had to deal with these aspects.

What We want to say to you is that this was never the intention for this planet. Never. This planet, that was created by the exhalation of Source and is an expression of the Divine Feminine, was never intended to become an experience based on lower energy expressions. This planet was intended for a different energy experience.

What occurred to taint the very existence of this planet was the corruption of the Divine Energy. The energy was manipulated by powerful beings whose intention was to destroy rather than create. You were never meant to experience this planet in a negative way. Yet, when the planet became captive to the darker forces, their manipulation and control of the resources resulted in a miserable existence for most humans.

The existence was so despicable that many of you offered your very soul for food, water, shelter, medicine, protection, friendship, and the big one, love. You bartered for a better way of living by appealing to the people of power at that time, thus accruing karma and soul contracts that took lifetimes to repay. Do you understand? Your way of life was often so meagre that your free will choice resulted in you adding up karmic debt. We will offer an example.

During one lifetime, you were a peasant ruled by an overlord that treated its tenants very cruelly. The crops you grew went to the overlord to feed his troops or guards. You were often hungry, and your children may have been sickly. During one season, you refused to hand over three-quarters of your harvest; your family needed the food. The overlord was not pleased and thrashed you. You, in a fit of anger, killed him with a pitchfork, and, in retaliation, you were killed.

In this scenario, the plight of you and your family, due to the greed of the overlord, led you to commit the act of taking another soul's life. Thus, you accrued karma and had to clear it. But you would not have had to accrue this karma if not for the greed of the overlord. There was enough harvest for him and for you, but his greed and sense of superiority caused him to demand more for him and his troops and less for you. Know that the overlord also accrued karma. His actions were not one of reverence for life. He was influenced by the hierarchy of power

CHAPTER SIXTEEN: THE IMPORTANCE OF CHOICE

before him and, instead of listening to his own sense of light and dark, he chose to become more of the latter. If he did not, he would have ended up poor, and that was not pleasant. Both the overlord and you (as the peasant) used free will decisions based on the current external environment. The way of living on your planet was, and is, very much imbalanced, and it was deliberately made so.

Life was hard for many. If you did not have wealth, then you more than likely were at the mercy of the hierarchy, and your existence appeared doomed. To avoid such a life, many of you bargained for a better existence through deals and agreements that bound you to countless lives on the planet.

Let Us repeat this truth to you again: life upon this planet was never intended to be experienced in such a traumatic manner. Your reality has been cleverly manipulated and subverted to hold you in more of a prison mode. Now, We solemnly ask you, do you think there are enough resources for all? Do you feel that the distribution of wealth and power is very uneven? Do you feel the greed of a minority is fair?

If you answered *yes* to any of the above, then the next question you may ask is *why*? In order to answer this, We encourage you to go deep within yourself to find the answer. To assist you, We will offer this question, 'How is it that the minority seem to wield power over the majority, and how do they do this?'.

We also encourage you to talk to others about this. We have noticed that single individuals who come together and unite their energy and intention are capable of great power. How this power is used is dependent on the consciousness of the group.

Let Us continue the discussion. The corruption of the planet has affected every soul that chose to experience an existence here. The subversive energy cleverly manipulated your free will and encouraged you to bind each other to soul contracts and karma. It encouraged you to dabble in lower vibrational energies to have control over others. This is where the term black magic and dark arts comes into play. Many of you freely chose to use lower vibrational forms of energy to manipulate and control. These energies became imprinted in your energy fields and were passed down from generation to generation. The corruptive energy would trigger the lower vibrational energy signatures in your auric field and create chaos in your life. The more chaos in your life, the more fearful you became, and the more you bargained for a better existence.

And so, again and again, you chose to reincarnate here and, again and again, the old energy manipulated you to quickly forget who you are and what you came to do. It

CHAPTER SIXTEEN: THE IMPORTANCE OF CHOICE

encouraged you to seek the more painful life experiences on the pretence that it would lead to freedom, when, in fact, it led to slavery. You became enslaved to a power outside yourself, and you forgot to become your own Divine power.

Now, there have been many souls that have chosen a more public platform to wake people up. You may be familiar with the names of Jesus, Martin Luther King, and Gandhi, but you also are aware of their demise. This was done on purpose, to squelch any thought of an uprising or a desire to come into your own power. It created hope and then fear. Hope (the higher vibrational energy form) was, more or less, quickly displaced by fear (the thought form that the old energy identified with). The fear was much longer lasting and much grander in scale than hope or even love. Fear was manipulated to become great and influential in every aspect of your life. You were manipulated to believe that fear was a more familiar feeling, and you had no choice but to live in fear. Fear of losing your job, fear of failing, fear of rejection, fear of abandonment, fear of poverty, fear of loss, and fear of death.

How are you doing? Do you feel the need to stop for a while and refocus? Do you feel that you have to integrate this a bit more? If so, take a rest. Put the book down.

CHAPTER SEVENTEEN

How to Release Soul Contracts and Karma

Welcome back. Did you rest for a while? Did you put the book down for a day, a week, a month, or longer? Or have you chosen to read on? Are you still curious as to what other information We may impart? Let Us further discuss soul contracts and karma.

We understand that currently many of you are still retaining the imprints of agreements made over the course of lifetimes,

CHAPTER SEVENTEEN: HOW TO RELEASE SOUL CONTRACTS AND KARMA

which are still affecting you at some level. We also know that it is necessary for them to be shifted and released once and for all.

The wonderful news is that this can be accomplished right here and now, and We will explain how it is done.

With your divine spark relit, you are vibrating at a higher frequency, and, thus, you are now able to become an extension of the higher vibrational energy that is now flowing into the planet. It is because of this that you are able to shift and clear any soul contracts and karma you have chosen to accrue. Another significant fact is that you are also able to clear such aspects from the other souls you entered the agreements with. This is truly a wonderful thing and, more importantly, it has been decreed by Source that this can take place.

If you are ready to do so, then the following steps are necessary. It is a very simple process but very powerful. Remember that simplicity in most things can assist in allowing you to experience a freer life.

Choose a time that you will be undisturbed and not distracted by external sources.

Choose a place that feels right for you. We would encourage it to be outside, under a tree or in the garden. If you cannot be outside, bring the outside in. Have a flower, leaf, grass, stone, pebble, or even a bowl of water near you. We ask this because you are part of the Divine Earth, and it is helpful to have nature with you as you release. Also, know that as you release, you are helping to release the Earth as well. You and the planet are one. Gaia holds the imprints of each soul's karma and soul contracts, and, as you clear your own, you are literally clearing the planet!

Breathe in and out four times. With the in-breath, you are breathing in your divine essence, and, with the out-breath, you are exhaling everything you are not.

Place your hand directly under your heart. This is where your divine spark has been activated and where it is the most felt. We encourage you to feel a sense of heat or tingling here.

We encourage you to say something similar to the following, asking for karma and soul contracts to be cleared:

CHAPTER SEVENTEEN: HOW TO RELEASE SOUL CONTRACTS AND KARMA

I, (your name), ask that from this moment on I become free of all past soul contracts, karma, and other forms of agreement that I entered into. I ask that this be lifted from me so that I can experience true freedom for myself and this planet. I freely hand this over to Source and divinely trust that this is now done.

Feel a sense of lightness come into your being. Tune into your physical self and be aware of certain sensations such as a tingling or warmth. You may feel peaceful and relaxed.

We now encourage you to rest for a while. This will be helpful in allowing the energy to integrate. We also encourage you to become aware of your everyday interactions and how you feel about certain moments in your life. We especially ask you to take note of how you react and feel to the more stressful encounters. If you feel more balanced during these times and are less reactive, then this is a very positive outcome.

CHAPTER EIGHTEEN

The Influence of Technology

Now that your divine spark has been activated and you are consciously aware of yourself and your surroundings, there are a few things that can be done to enhance your way of life.

Remember that you are a very powerful being. You are a part of Source and, as such, you are a powerful co-creator. You are no longer here to be manipulated and fed information that encourages the loss of personal power; you are consciously deciding to attract and receive information that leads you to reinforce how powerful you are.

CHAPTER EIGHTEEN: THE INFLUENCE OF TECHNOLOGY

This can be achieved by more positive self-expression. You are a unique and dynamic human being who is capable of great love and kindness. You are here at this time on the planet to break free of all past conditioning that has led you to believe you are anything less than a co-creator of Source. You are up for the job. You have earned the right to be here at this time and in this moment. You are ready to break free of all restraints and, in turn, help others to break free of their outdated beliefs that have enslaved them.

This you will do in a loving and thoughtful manner. You will lead by example and the utter conviction of who you truly are. This is the expression of personal power. We encourage you to speak and think kindlier of yourself so that your unique power is attractive to others and they will want what you have and be encouraged to seek it.

We encourage you to be less distracted by devices, which can occupy much of your free time if you allow it. The many devices on this planet seek to disrupt the neurological pathways of the brain and steal away your awareness of what is happening within the body. Your physical body is a wonderful vehicle, and it has a life force and a functioning of its own. It is essential to listen to it.

Your inner awareness can communicate through the body. It can give you guidance in regard to what feels right and what does not. Do you recall times when you have literally felt your stomach drop at certain news that has been delivered to you? Or when you have goose bumps or that tingling feeling? These are examples of a level of communication felt by your inner awareness that has been communicated via the body. Do not ignore these feelings. These are insights and signposts for you to heed and follow. We say to you that many times during the course of your day, your body is sending signals to you in an effort to guide you. Playing on smartphones, computers, and other electronic devices disrupts the signals in your body, creating confusion and unquiet. These devices seek to reinforce separation from yourself. With the relighting of your divine spark, you will feel less inclined to be distracted by electronics. We ask that you follow this disinclination and see it for what it is.

We also wish to impress upon you the need for sleep. We have noticed that many of you retire to bed very late, often after exposure to computer and television viewings. As We have mentioned, if you choose to play on devices before sleep, this will send disruptive signals through the body and, in particular, to the brain. For your body to rest and recover, there needs to be a period of calming before you retire. We would encourage you to read a book (one that evokes pleasurable feelings rather than the opposite), chat, play cards or games, anything that does not require a device. If you wind down naturally for one hour before

CHAPTER EIGHTEEN: THE INFLUENCE OF TECHNOLOGY

bed, then your sleep pattern will be enhanced, and there will be more vigour in your body.

We would also encourage you to not have electronics in your bedroom. It is important for there to be the least amount of disturbance as possible. As you sleep, you dream. The dream state is an important time for your body and your soul. This is a time of healing and information. It is a time when an answer to a conundrum may be given and, most importantly, an intention for the coming day can be set.

In the past, before the emergence of the new energy, it was possible that the dreamtime states of many of you were able to be tampered with. Remember, the previous energy was about corruption and powerlessness, and it was automatically drawn to anything that threatened it. When you enter a state of dreaming, this is an opportunity for you to meet with your guides and your Higher Self, and to receive healing and information. We encourage you to ensure that you are always shielded and guarded by the higher realms of light. This is particularly important as you sleep. As you slumber you can be vulnerable to lower vibrational energies that may scramble your energy field. To avoid this, the intention of being guarded at all times is suggested.

The presence of computers in your bedroom and the busyness of the mind before you go to sleep means that you are unable to receive the full benefit of healing and information that awaits you at that level. Thus, you may awaken with feelings of heaviness and unease. The intention you may have set for the coming day, week, or months is compromised, and you may feel disillusioned that you are not making headway with a problem you have been seeking an answer to. This is solely because your system is unable to remember the answer and bring it forth from the dream state to your reality.

Does this make sense? Do you feel the ring of truth in these words? Do you feel that you spend too much of your time on devices? Are you reluctant to reduce the time you spend on these electronics? If so, We say that this is a good thing to recognise. We also encourage you to place the book down for a while and sit with these feeling of reluctance to part with any electronics.

We ask that you place your hand on your heart where your divine spark sits and consciously ask for assistance in reducing the need for electronics. Consciously ask for a restful dream state where you can take full advantage of all that is offered during this time. You may feel a stirring on this part of your body as you ask for this. Your divine spark always seeks to empower you. Trust it for it is the truest form of you.

CHAPTER NINETEEN

The Source Chakra

We have been discussing your state of being. We have suggested that you have more positive self-talk and to decrease mind-stimulating electronics. Now, We will talk about the very special gift that Source has given to humans at this time. Indeed, We have been saving the best 'til last!

We will discuss chakras with you now. Are you aware that the imprints of past lives, karma, and soul contracts are held within the chakras? Do you realise that, during this current life, all the above is held by all the chakras first and foremost? Are you aware that as you die, the chakras release all the information and experiences of your life and previous lives and transforms this data into an energy?

All the information was collected from every chakra as you died and then stored in a prism-shaped object that is unique to you. When you chose to reincarnate back to this planet, the prism is opened, and the information is transferred to the chakras of your physical body.

To reiterate: the chakras are the energy centres of the body. You are no doubt familiar with the seven major ones: *The Base, Sacral, Solar Plexus, Heart, Throat, Third Eye, and Crown.* You may also be familiar with the chakras located at the bottom of your feet, hands, ears, behind your knees, and in the crease of your elbow. We ask that you become familiar and pay attention to these chakras more than ever before as they are holding an energy unlike humankind has ever experienced. With the lighting of the divine spark, the chakras have also been relit and illuminated. There has even been the introduction of an extra chakra to the human experience.

This chakra, known as the Source Chakra, is now the driving force for all your chakras. It is an overseer. It is a stabiliser. It seeks only to heal and to love, and it can never be corrupted or deactivated whilst you are in human form. When you die, unlike the other chakras that dissolve into themselves, the Source Chakra will leave you and return to Source itself.

CHAPTER NINETEEN: THE SOURCE CHAKRA

This chakra is pure Source energy and, although very small in size, it contains an enormous amount of energy that is undiluted and pure. This chakra is located near the heart chakra and has been given to humans to strengthen the emotion of unconditional love. Unconditional love is what Source is. It is what humans, and most other beings, seek to be and to become. This love is what is needed to recreate your planet and to finally bring about the transformation.

The most marvellous gift of all is that the Source Chakra was given to you at the start of the book. Remember how We said that this is an energy book? One of the main intentions of this book is to facilitate the receiving of this chakra. What is even more exciting is that, as you have received this chakra into your being, you are now able to facilitate the giving of this chakra to those around you. This encompasses those you love including your animal companions. Source loves every one of Its creations equally, and thus, all flora and fauna and everything in between have this extra chakra.

So, with the knowledge that you now have an extra special chakra, We ask that you tend to your chakras daily. This will only take a few minutes and, as you get into the practice of attending to your chakras, you will quickly fall into a routine.

Here is an outline of how to attend to your chakras:

Place your hand near your heart area, and call on your divine spark.

Ask that your chakras are balanced and in a healthy state.

Ask that you be made aware of any chakras that may need attending to and what is required to return normalcy.

Say, 'Thank you'.

CHAPTER NINETEEN: THE SOURCE CHAKRA

You may develop your own way of attending to your chakras, and this is also good. The point is that you are aware of your chakras and the importance they play in helping you to be a more powerful you.

CHAPTER TWENTY

Tending Your Aura

We will now discuss your aura, which is your energy field. It is an extension of you. It can be invisible to most humans, but certain imaging machines are used to show your aura. Your aura can consist of different colours depending on your state of being.

Your aura is constantly changing and is very responsive to your surroundings. It will automatically make itself bigger in situations that require you to command a more powerful presence, such as when you need to speak your truth or when you are entering a social gathering that requires the mingling of different energies. The addition

CHAPTER TWENTY: TENDING YOUR AURA

of the Source Chakra enables your aura to be in tune with what is best for you at all times.

We have noticed in the past that many of you carry within your own personal aura the energy of others you have unconsciously attracted and acquired. This means that you are the vehicle for other souls' angst, and you may experience feelings of confusion and tiredness that is not of your own making. If this energy is not removed, over time it can impact on your well-being, especially when it comes to brain and emotional health. It is not healthy to carry the energy of others within your own unique being, whether you have chosen this unconsciously or consciously. This has been a part of your conditioning and desire to help others.

We say this to you: if you desire to help others, then only carry and be responsible for your own energy. Tend to your aura as you would a garden or a home. Clean it out regularly. Give it a weekly vacuum or weeding. Polish it or rake it regularly. Ensure it is loved and maintained as it is a unique extension of you and contains your own unique signature that cannot be forged. Remember, highly evolved beings look at your aura, not your physical features. Your physical features are a hazy blur to Us, but your aura is clear and tells Us much about who you are.

Your aura has the imprints of your past lives on this planet, and the past lives you have spent in other dimensions and timelines. Your aura tells of your own unique experiences and can hold the hurts and the triumphs of this current life within it. Your aura is another form of your consciousness, and it has served as your undoing on some level in the past. This is why We encourage you to become aware of your aura and tend to it regularly.

In the past, your aura, much like most of everything on this planet, was corrupted and tainted. We have indicated that your aura contains your current life experiences within it, both the joys and the joylessness. In the past, the controlling energy encouraged your joyless experiences to be activated and heightened within your aura so that you were mainly influenced by these experiences, which allowed you to become stuck in a victim mentality. As you became a victim, you attracted victims and victim experiences to you.

Your aura acts like a magnet. It can attract joy and pain. If the joyless experiences and emotions are heightened and active, then there will be a steady flow of experiences in this form that confirm it. Therefore, it is important that you are aware of the state of your aura on most days.

We will offer an example. You wake up in a grumpy mood. Your aura reflects this energy of grumpiness. You are late for work or school. As the day progresses, you find that you have interactions with grumpy people and everything seems to be going wrong. You lose your pen, forget that you

CHAPTER TWENTY: TENDING YOUR AURA

have a meeting, you get more work pushed onto you. Does this sound familiar? Your aura, which is an extension and reflection of you, is a magnet. It is actively inviting fewer positive experiences to happen to you. If you continue to be grumpy for a longer period of time, then your life will be grumpy. What is needed is for you to reset yourself. You can do this very quickly. Simply call forth the energy of your divine spark, and ask that it clears the grumpiness from your energy field. Breath in and out several times. It will be done. Now, you will be more balanced and be less affected by the day's activities. You will find that your day improves. You are in charge of your reality! You have consciously activated the energy within your body, and the Source Chakra allows this to happen quickly and effectively.

You may be thinking that this sounds too easy. We say that easy is the new way forward for you. Simplicity in all things is very powerful. Try out Our suggestion.

With the assistance of the Source Chakra and your connection with the emergent energy, you can hold more positive imprints within your own aura that will attract positive experiences into your life. It also means you will be aware of when you take on another person's energy. When this occurs, you may feel imbalanced. You may question why you feel tired or lethargic. Beforehand, you would not have been quite so aware. You would have been stumbling around with many different energies within your own aura, which were counter-productive to your own being.

So, once again, We say to you: tend to your aura. Be aware of it, and ensure it is the exact fit for you each day. Visualise any colour that comes to mind as you think of your aura and allow it to settle around you. Your aura can be a different colour or be a combination of different colours every day. It's much like you choosing an outfit! Have fun with your aura. Dress it up, make it sparkle. Add your shield and sword to it if you feel like it.

Just as your aura is an extension of you, so is the grounding cord that links you to the planet at this time. Your grounding cord is a line of energy that extends from your Base Chakra to the Earth. It is a form of attachment to this planet originally intended to connect you with the unique Divine Feminine energy so you could co-create with Her in a balanced and divine way. Once you transitioned from the Earth, the grounding cord was freed and returned back to the Earth. Therefore, this energy cord is the energy of the Divine Earth Mother.

Once again, as with your aura, your grounding cord was defiled and subverted so it became more of a chain and anchor to the planet. Your Base Chakra is important in helping you live on the planet. Instead of being balanced, this chakra turned into a high spinning vortex of fear and confusion. This

CHAPTER TWENTY: TENDING YOUR AURA

meant that the connection with the Earth was compromised, and you felt disconnected from the planet. With this loss of connection came the loss of nurture for the Earth and, thus, the ravaging of the planet came into being. We have watched from afar as humans mindlessly polluted and killed the precious eco-systems that were created by Mother Earth, and We have watched your Base and Sacral Chakras suffer the same. Both these chakras became very fear-based, and they were used to control and for you to be controlled by others.

Understand that the controlling energy manipulated these two chakras very well. As you came from a place of fear, then fearful situations came into being on a massive scale. Wars were created from both the Base and Sacral Chakra. All forms of fighting come from this fear, whether on a global or a more personal scale. Most importantly, it impacted Mother Earth as She became a victim of this fear.

We have said that the grounding cord is part of the Earth's energy. Therefore, it stands to reason that as each soul suffered, their suffering was felt by the Earth. As many billions of souls constantly suffer, the need for action to change this was of paramount importance to Source, who understood that Mother Earth was breaking apart and would soon be destroyed. As powerful as She is, even She has Her limits, and Her call for help was heeded by the Creator. And so, beings like Us have been assisting Her and Her inhabitants.

And now, with the emergence of the new energy, your grounding cords are being returned to their original intention. We ask that you be aware of it and visualise this cord extending from your base chakra to the Earth. This will assist you to be connected both to the Earth and the Sky.

CHAPTER TWENTY-ONE

The Multiverse

This now brings Us to the topic of the Multiverse. We say this to you now: be aware that you are living in a Multiverse rather than a universe. The term universe was coined millennia ago to mislead you into thinking that there is simply one universe that exists. This is not the truth. Your Earth is part of a much more extensive and expansive Multiverse that is beyond your mortal comprehension and belief system.

The controlling energy was very good at helping you feel confined and three-dimensional. It encouraged you to rely on the five senses only. It discouraged you from using what you named the sixth sense. You are aware that this sixth sense can be described as a feeling. It could be a feeling that something was not quite right and, thus, served as a warning system. Or it could be a positive feeling and, thus, served as a confirmation that all will be well. You have heard the phrase, 'I just had this feeling that something was not quite right'. All this means is that you tuned into the vibration and something did not resonate within you. It was a disharmonious feeling. You might not be aware of why you felt like that, but just because you do not know where something comes from does not mean that you should discredit the feeling altogether. Yet time and time again, you did not trust this inner sense. Instead, you relied on what you heard or what you saw, and many times it backfired and left you feeling fearful and even more distrusting. The old energy loved this. It tried to disconnect you from your own intuition and gut instinct. It encouraged you to fully invest your energy into what was presented right in front of you.

The controlling energy encouraged you to believe that there is only one universe. If you were lucky and fortunate enough to be more informed that something may exist outside this planet and outside your experience of life, then it tried to limit your access to this as well.

Each and every one of you has access to the Multiverses and to a plethora of information, for each universe was

CHAPTER TWENTY-ONE: THE MULTIVERSE

created at a different frequency and, as such, holds different data.

Are you aware that you can now access many universes to obtain information? This is why We encourage you to tend your aura and check your grounding cord daily. These two energy embodiments are your keys to time travelling and information gathering. You can especially utilise the Multiverse as you sleep. Simply state the intention that you wish to obtain information, healing, transformation, and guidance from the most suitable universe for your requirements. You will be amazed at what you discover, how far you can travel, and what energy beings you can encounter on the journey.

No longer can you be restricted to the one universe that holds some information but not all of it. You have a choice of universes, and remember: each universe is solely created to align with your intention. Each of the universes is neutral in their energy and will be more readily accessible and align more strongly when you have positive intentions rather than the opposite. While you are in mortal form, this is how the Multiverse works. Once you transition into the non-physical, then your relationship with the Multiverse will become very different.

Now, let Us return to the name you have coined the sixth sense. We encourage this sense or feeling to be known as the Source Sense, and We would like for you to truly hone it as much as you are able. The more you trust and use this energy, the more you will grow in spiritual evolution whilst you are on the planet. Understand that the new energy is very much about assisting you to create a happier state of being. This is made easier with the gift of the Source Chakra.

We would also encourage you to connect with the stars and to observe the night sky on a regular basis. The night sky awakens certain sensory receptors in your body and has the ability to help you feel that you are part of something that is much greater than yourself.

You may also discover that the night sky is full of activities you may not have observed before! The same can be said of the daytime sky. Look more to the skies and observe what is happening. We notice that many people walk around distracted by their devices and pay the Earth and sky very little attention. We say to you that there is a lot happening that is not necessarily in your best interests yet it is right in front of you! Please be aware of this.

CHAPTER TWENTY-TWO

How to Release Karma

The Source Chakra is an amazing gift. It helps you connect with an energy that is infinitely more powerful than your human consciousness can imagine.

For so long, you have been encouraged and brainwashed into believing you are powerless and worth virtually nothing unless you have an outward show of wealth. This may equate to a good job, fancy car, a comfortable and even grandiose home, smart clothes, or expensive accessories. Many of you, over countless lives, have fought to have material wealth that allowed for a certain degree of security for you and your loved ones.

Many of you have transitioned with a belief mindset that the more wealth you accumulate, the more powerful you will be, and you did not care what you did to ensure you received it. In fact, so powerful was your belief that the outer world was infinitely more powerful than the inner world, it became heavily imprinted in your DNA. This was passed along to any offspring you sired during your many lives and influenced that child's mindset to believe that wealth was of the utmost importance. This genetic imprinting made it incredibly easy for you to be manipulated by the controlling energy that eagerly fed this thought system and helped you create an existence based on struggle and disconnection.

Are you able to recall such times when you felt you had no other option but to commit an action that went against how you truly felt about the situation? Did you stand aside and watch a school child bullied by another student? Did you make fun of anyone that had a less than pleasing appearance? Did you steal money or property from your parents, grandparents, friend, or relative in order to buy something you felt you could not live without? Have you taken something from a shop on a dare? Did you experience sex when you were not ready because other people had and you felt left out?

CHAPTER TWENTY-TWO: HOW TO RELEASE KARMA

These are examples of actions in your life that have resulted in karma, soul contracts, and you giving away your power. We have used some common behaviours to illustrate Our point. We are aware that many of you have committed actions upon yourself that are far more severe than these examples and had far reaching consequences on your personal being. Regardless of what occurred, any damage to your being, physically, emotionally, and spiritually, is of great distress to Us and to Source.

This brings Us back to the Source Chakra and the gift this chakra brings to humanity. We invite you to write, or voice record, the instances in your life where you acted against your sense of knowing, which in turn created another cycle of debts owed to other persons. This need not be a detailed description of what transpired as all that is required is for these experiences to be bought to your consciousness to allow the full release of these experiences.

After you have taken a moment to record your experiences, it is time for you to release them now and forever.

The process is very simple and personal, and there is no right way or wrong way to do it. Remember that intention is all that is required.

We encourage you to find a nice place and strongly urge you do not have any electronic device on your person or, if possible, in the place you choose to experience this release. Sitting in nature would be wonderful.

1) Breathe in and out as many times as you like until your mind becomes settled and you are at ease within yourself.
2) Call on the Source Chakra and try and tune into it as much as you are able.
3) Ask the Source Chakra to clear all the chakras in your body from all forms of soul contracts, karma, and anything else that may hold a sense of fear and loss of power.
4) Feel the energy of the Source Chakra sweeping through the chakras effortlessly and quickly. Notice any changes in your body such as alternate hot and cold feelings, tingling, vibrations, or any sounds, such as music, that you may hear.
5) Feel yourself becoming lighter and calmer. There may even be the beginnings of a smile upon your lips as your physical body responds to the changes.
6) Allow this process to continue for as long as necessary. You will know when it is complete.
7) Express your gratitude to Source.

You are able to use this process as many times as you feel is necessary during the course of your life. It is

CHAPTER TWENTY-TWO: HOW TO RELEASE KARMA

especially helpful when you have had a disagreement with someone that has rattled your inner being.

If you are unable to feel any change in your physical being this does not mean there is nothing happening. We assure you there is, and We encourage you to do this as often as required.

During times of stress and emotional upheavals, this release process is enormously helpful and will not only centre you but transmute any energy you may have attracted to yourself from other people. This way, you can be sure that the energy you are feeling is your own and not somebody else's you have taken on.

The Source Chakra is amazing at clearing any emotional dross, and We encourage you to use it.

CHAPTER TWENTY-THREE

The Positive Changes

It is Our intention that you will now have the ability to experience your current life in a much more positive and joyful way. We have previously spoken about the fact that at times you may feel sad, angry, hurt, and fearful; this is part of the human experience on this planet. The truth is that you will not now become these experiences and will no longer continue feeling that a happier state of being is near impossible.

What will happen is that you will begin to co-create with the Earth and transform this planet to its original state of being. This is very important for you to understand.

CHAPTER TWENTY-THREE: THE POSITIVE CHANGES

Instead of being manipulated to work against the planet in a more destructive form, you will automatically begin to look for ways to support the planet in a constructive way. You will find yourself being more Earth conscious. If you are already deeply connected to the planet, then ideas will flow easily to you, and you will attract other souls who can assist in bringing these ideas to fruition.

Now, let Us briefly touch on some positive changes that can be offered to humanity should they want them. We will mention this briefly, but know that We will elaborate more on these changes in due course.

In the future, there will be an emergence of community-based concepts. Retreats and centres will come into being that draw large gatherings of highly motivated people to come and co-create together. There will also be the presence of inter-dimensional energy beings (like Us) who will offer their services to help rebuild the planet. We will not remain hidden but, instead, be in plain sight. The intention of these gatherings is to bring forth ideas and technology that will co-create with the Earth energy and restore health to the planet.

For the planet to flourish, there will be the introduction of new food sources that are easily cultivated and nutritious. You may be drawn to a plant-based diet that is full of goodness and nutrition and will serve the functioning of the human body effectively. We have observed many of you are already on the path of a plant-based diet, and We are happy for you. We also know that many of you cannot go without meat for you feel too ill when you do. This is because the meat you have eaten has been drugged and, therefore, your body has become addicted to it. This has been done deliberately, and We understand how difficult this is for you.

There will also be offerings of new technology that will support the rebuilding of Earth. Some of this technology will focus on bringing health to you. We can see that many are suffering and ailing from various poisons that have accumulated in the body. These poisons have also affected the functioning of your mind and brain. Therefore, first and foremost, the focus will be on restoring good health. We also observe that many are functioning at less than 50% of your vital capacity and Our intention is to restore you to 100% of your vitality. As your health returns, you will find more vigour to assist in the restoration of the planet at all levels.

With your health being a primary focus for Us, We will offer healing chambers that can restore your vital capacity. If you freely choose to restore your health, then this will be forthcoming. If some souls choose to decline this offer, then We will support those people as much as We can, using foods and other methods that will be effective but

CHAPTER TWENTY-THREE: THE POSITIVE CHANGES

take much longer to eventuate. As always, the choice is yours, and We respect it.

We have also observed that with the decline of a healthy body and brain function, there are associated behaviours. We understand that many of you experience mood disorders that impact greatly on, not only yourself, but the ones that care deeply for you. Anger, rage, fear, and disassociation from self are just a few examples of self-destructive behaviours that have plagued the planet for many, many years. Help in restoring these imbalances will be offered.

It has been decreed that this planet is to be restored to balance, and this means that souls living on this planet are to be balanced as well. There is no room for the emergence of anger and hostility that were rife on this planet for thousands of years. It simply will not occur.

This brings Us to the matter of human emotions that are so wondrous to Us in all their healthy expressions. Again, We repeat: while you are human, you will experience emotions that can be fear-based such as pain and anxiety. What you will not do is become this experience and create your life from this experience. A new form of technology will be offered that will, again, be in the form of chambers. These chambers will be solely used for the purpose of balancing all fear-based emotion that may arise in your life.

Say, for example, you have a disagreement with another, you cannot seem to find a resolution between yourselves, and it is creating a sense of imbalance. A special chamber will be available for you to seek and find a resolution to any perceived problem that may take time to be resolved. The chambers will facilitate and, most of all, ensure that a peaceful outcome is made that suits all parties. Any energy of anger and fear that may arise will be quickly transmuted. These chambers will contain the energy of Source and Gaia. Such is the power and love that is offered here, problems will be quickly and lovingly resolved.

Most importantly, these chambers will facilitate decisions of spokespeople that wish to implement new ideas, new creations, and new thoughts. As these chambers will not tolerate falsehoods or ideas that are not in alignment with the new energy, ideas that flow forth will be created from a genuine desire to assist the planet and Her inhabitants. Needless to say, these chambers will vary in size and be freely and easily accessible to all souls. It will be up to the Earth's inhabitants as to how many and where these chambers will be.

Remember this technology is offered to you, but it is up to your free will as to the implementation of the offering.

As new technology is introduced, there will be a group of beings that will assist in the implementation of new

CHAPTER TWENTY-THREE: THE POSITIVE CHANGES

understandings. These beings are from the cosmos and will be the first of the extra-terrestrial energies that will introduce themselves. It is important to hold them in your vibration, welcome them to your planet, and ask for their assistance and healing technology. Remember, all beings that come to help are mindful of your free will and will not attempt to manipulate your choices in any way.

There will also be the emergence of other energies that will assist you in returning to your full power. These beings will be introduced in a gradual way so that there is not an overload of information, and the integration of a new state of being will flow.

We say to you: if anyone (human and non- human) attempts to interfere in your free will choices, either through manipulation or fear, be aware of their true motive. Use the divine spark to intuitively convey to you what, and who, to trust. The divine spark cannot be corrupted or manipulated and serves as a very good barometer of what is authentic and what is not.

CHAPTER TWENTY-FOUR

In Summary

We are now nearing the completion of *Spirit Talks One*. We trust that We have helped activate your understanding of who you really are. We hope We have helped you understand the power that you have as an individual. We wished to shed light on the fact that your reality has been cleverly manipulated and distorted to keep you feeling separate and absent from your divine energy.

Much damage has been done to the planet and its inhabitants, but this is coming to an end, and you are the bringer of change and light. Do not underestimate your power; endeavour to create an authentic life for yourself

CHAPTER TWENTY-FOUR: IN SUMMARY

and those around you. You have reignited your divine spark and have been gifted with the Source Chakra. As such, what you perceived as impossible or improbable no longer holds that same limiting vibration.

You are now more than capable of intending a happier and abundant life despite the turmoil and confusion that swirls around you. All you are called to do is step away from that energy and into your own uniqueness. You are the key to your success and happiness and, as such, you will be guided through situations that are no longer suitable for you. Now, more than ever before, trust your intuition. The new energy will support you. If you find it difficult to navigate your way through your reality despite your best intention, We promise that if you follow Our suggestions plus tap into your own unique abilities, the outcome will be a positive one.

In summation:

You are a unique expression of Source. Your uniqueness is your strength. Your planet was never intended to be a lower vibrational experience, but the corrupted energy manipulated your reality to be this way. Your divine spark has been relit, and you have been gifted with the Source Chakra. This means that you can more easily step into your power and begin to create a life based on your truth, not the falsehoods that have run your planet for aeons. You have the ability to clear all karmic debts and soul contracts in this very *NOW* moment by following Our suggestions and intending for this to happen.

Humanity's cry for help has been heard across the multiverses and many are waiting to assist you. Watch for them and be ready for the window of change when it occurs between 2013 and 2027 Earth years. *NOW* is the time to be awake and informed. Tend to your aura and grounding cord on a regular basis. They will assist you in staying grounded and balanced. Remember that too much time on electronics disturbs the frequency of your body. Use these devices with prudence.

Be aware of your free will choices and intend, intend, intend. Your conscious intention can be manifested more easily and quickly than ever before due to the new energy bathing the planet. Use it. Become it. Live it.

CHAPTER TWENTY-FIVE

One Last Word

You are souls of the Earth. You are an expression of the Creator who is trying to bring light to a planet that has been held captive for aeons. Time and time again, many of you have chosen to return to this planet to bring salvation, and, time and time again, you have been caught in the illusion and distracted from the truth. Such is the power of the individual soul, the darker energies have resorted to manipulating you on every level, from the physical to the spiritual. Yet, here you are. You are still plugging away to uncover your truth and the truth of the planet. You are ploughing through a toxic world filled with greed, corruption, lies and poison – everything that is the antithesis of who you really are!

Understand that you are a powerful force and, to negate that power, there has to be some very powerful forces in play to not only squelch your magnificence but to ensure that you never see the light of day again.

This is why *Spirit Talks One* book is being offered to you at this time. There is power in the simplicity of Our words, and it is directed at stirring up your unique energy frequency. We encourage you to question and to have conversations amongst yourselves, for this is how answers will be found. Know that as you gather together, We will also be present, for this is Our role now. To most We are an unseen force, but truly know that We are very real and a part of your human journey.

You have accessed this book, and that is the most important step. It is the stepping stone to freedom, and, in that freedom, you have the opportunity to marvel at who you are. We encourage you to often connect with the Creator. The Source Chakra allows you to connect more easily, so use this gift!

Test it out. Test Us out. We have observed that humans enjoy testing things including other humans. It helps to appease the ego which is always questioning and wondering. So, go ahead. Test Us. Ask Us. We will

CHAPTER TWENTY-FIVE: ONE LAST WORD

do Our utmost to pass these tests, if they are within the realms of your free will and your highest good. As We have explained, We are here to assist. We are a team member, wanting to achieve the best and richest outcome for us all.

Know that this is the first book in a series of three. In the next book, We will offer information about the older energy and the beings who chose to control and manipulate it. We did not delve into this too deeply in *Spirit Talks One* for, presently, this is enough information for you to integrate.

Until then, Our intention for you is simply this: Wake up and have the intention to help others to wake up. Arising from your mind-induced slumber is the only way to bring changes to this wonderful planet, and it is literally time for you to rise and shine!

We also encourage you to do your own research regarding the history of the planet. Perhaps begin with the Sumerians and discover what knowledge they held and the inventions they bought forth. These inventions are still being used in your present day.

We also say to you that not everyone will want to wake up and be more informed. We have stated that it requires a certain level of the populace to shift their consciousness to create positive change, and this is well on its way to occurring. We encourage you to be discerning with your energy when it comes to helping people to wake up. Some souls will not want to. Even with the relighting of their divine spark and the gift of the Source Chakra, if their free will is not to shift consciousness, then there is very little you can do to change this. The time for devoting much of your energy to showing them why they are encouraged to wake up and the steps to this freedom has now waned. Rather, this period in your planet's history is geared towards your own enlightenment and attracting similar enlightened souls to hold the new frequency. We encourage you to try and assist the wakening process, but at the same time, know when to move on and away from people that are resistant to your energy and knowledge. Instead, you can help them on another level by having the intention that they receive understanding if they so choose. This is when beings like Ourselves will step in and be at the ready should they wish to change. This is one of the ways We are assisting you currently, so please use Us!

Thank you for choosing to receive Our offering of *Spirit Talks One*. We look forward to further discussions in *Spirit Talks Two*.

Until then, We remain yours in Spirit.
-The Collective

About Paulette

Born in Adelaide, South Australia, Paulette has been conversing with Spirit ever since she was a young child, which made life simultaneously interesting and tricky.

It was not until she was forty that she made the conscious decision to integrate Spirit more into her life and stop hiding her ability to communicate with them.

As a result, from 2007 to 2012 Paulette held fortnightly meditation evenings called 'An Evening with Gaia'. However, at the close of 2012, Spirit advised Paulette that the meditations had run their course.

From 2012 to the present day, Paulette has concentrated on individual healing sessions and studying Bioresonance Therapy. She works full time as a bioresonance practitioner and facilitates 'Spirit Talk' sessions, where she channels information from *The Collective* to small group of individuals.

This is her first foray into the literary world, and she hopes this book will bring light and knowledge to all who read it. Find out more about Paulette at spirittalks.com.au.

How I connect with Spirit

Kylie —

At the age of 29, I embarked on my spiritual journey. It began with daily meditation, mystery school studies, and lots, and lots of reading. Over the years, my connection to Spirit has refined and strengthened through trust, understanding of self, and awareness of my connection to all things great and small. It is now a part of my every day. Sometimes it can be a feeling, a smell or a strong instinct; other times it will be an overwhelming thought or audible message. Spirit often chooses recurring numbers to communicate, and nature and animals are very strong message bearers for me also. Whether I'm working with a client, out in nature, or going about my day, if I feel an overwhelming sense of heartfelt emotions, I know Spirit is close. With love and gratitude, I acknowledge Spirit daily through thought and often out aloud, 'Thank you. I love you guys.'

Helen —
I am an Integrated Therapist that includes professional and spiritual counselling, Theta healing, and kinesiology. I focus on activating and stimulating my client's energy flow, helping them to release blocks on all levels. This helps to create major change in the client's body, mind, and emotions. I simply allow Spirit to flow through me and assist me with each person. I trust the energy in all of my sessions and do not question. I have found this to be the key in my personal communication with Spirit. I see myself as a doorway and Spirit as the key for my client's transformation. Together, we provide the best outcome for each unique soul.

Lynda —
Once the stories of myself wore away, which took time and wasn't easy, what was present was something else. This something is not this, not that, not a thing. It is inside, beside, around, through and in between everything that exists, me included. It is endless and always here to be engaged with. My logical mind has a field day with not knowing while acknowledging the knowing of it at the same time. I can't deny where I find myself. Here, as part of, this. It isn't mine, this all. I still remain a flawed human with lots of room for improvement! What's different

is I allow, this. I notice, this. It has nothing to do with me, Lynda, but comes through this me that I am. I see it, I am in awe of it. As in quantum physics, there is a recognisable space from where everything arises from, this is spirit. We are all part of this. No exception.

How I connect with Spirit

www.ingramcontent.com/pod-product-compliance
Lightning Source LLC
Chambersburg PA
CBHW050554300426
44112CB00013B/1908